THE ROAD TO
BAMA

THE ROAD TO
BAMA

Incredible Twists and Improbable Turns
Along the Crimson Tide Recruiting Trail

Andrew J. Bone
with Tom VanHaaren

TRIUMPH
BOOKS

Library of Congress Cataloging-in-Publication Data
Names: Bone, Andrew J., author. | VanHaaren, Tom, author.
Title: The road to Bama : incredible twists and improbable turns along the Crimson
    Tide recruiting trail / Andrew J. Bone with Tom VanHaaren.
Description: Chicago, Illinois : Triumph Books, [2020] | Summary: "This book is
    full of stories of Alabama recruited its star players to its football team"
    —Provided by publisher.
Identifiers: LCCN 2020018421 (print) | LCCN 2020018422 (ebook) |
    ISBN 9781629378077 (paperback) | ISBN 9781641255028 (epub)
Subjects: LCSH: University of Alabama—Football. | High school athletes—
    Recruiting—United States.
Classification: LCC GV958.A4 B66 2020 (print) | LCC GV958.A4 (ebook) |
    DDC 796.332/630976184—dc23
LC record available at https://lccn.loc.gov/2020018421
LC ebook record available at https://lccn.loc.gov/2020018422

This book is available in quantity at special discounts for your group or organization. For further information, contact:

Triumph Books LLC
814 North Franklin Street
Chicago, Illinois 60610
(312) 337-0747
www.triumphbooks.com

Printed in U.S.A.
ISBN: 978-1-62937-807-7
Design by Preston Pisellini

*To my father, who defeated Stage 4 Colon Cancer in 2012.
To two of my best friends, Jason and Jeff, who are also
currently battling cancer. We pray for you guys every day.
My mom—everything you have done for me. To my wife,
Audrey, thank you for the endless support and love!*

—A.B.

Contents

Foreword

The memories are still so fresh. I was a 5-year-old, Little League football player in Trussville, Alabama. Our games that fall were in the morning, and as soon as the game ended, I'd sprint to my dad's Chevrolet Caprice Classic. Jerome Barker, my father, always parked as close to the football field as he could because he knew we had to get out of there as fast as possible. He understood we had precious little time to reach our destination 15 miles away: Legion Field.

Even as a 5 year old, I felt the rush of adrenaline the first time I walked into the stadium that was swallowed whole by a Crimson-clad mass. Holding my dad's hand, I looked down at the field—that magical field—and that's when the dream was planted: I wanted to be the quarterback for Alabama.

Over my teenage years, my dad and I kept going to Legion Field. I sold Cokes in the upper deck. I swore to myself that one day I'd be Alabama's starting quarterback, but I was a late bloomer. In the ninth grade, I stood only 5'4". By my senior year at Trussville High, I'd risen to six feet but only weighed 175 pounds. I was a beanpole of an 18 year old. Army and North Carolina State offered me football scholarships—to play free safety. Early in my senior year, I was crestfallen. I thought my football dream to play for Bama was dead.

Looking back, I needed someone like Andrew Bone to scout me. I had a big game my senior year against Mountain Brook. That is where it all began for me as a quarterback prospect. It took coach Pat Sullivan seeing me play that night against his son, Patrick, to begin to get recognition from other schools. To put it another way, it took an Auburn coach to get me to Alabama. It's crazy that I ended up being helped by the rival school. Suddenly, Florida State's Bobby Bowden offered me a scholarship to play quarterback on the condition that I redshirt and ride the bench for a few years. But then it finally came: a scholarship offer from Alabama head coach Gene Stallings to play for the Tide. I sat in his office on a Sunday in January of 1990 and told him that I'd basically been a Bama commit since the age of 5.

So much has changed in the recruiting process/business since my senior year of high school in 1990. And right now there is no better recruiting analyst and recruiting reporter in the nation than Andrew. Shoot, I know coaches who call *him* for information. Even parents of players are constantly hounding him for insight. Andrew is as plugged in as anyone when it comes to all things Alabama football recruiting.

This is just one reason why I love *The Road to Bama: Incredible Twists and Improbable Turns Along the Crimson Tide Recruiting Trail*. Andrew comes on my radio show about once a week and talks eloquently about virtually every elite high school player in the nation. He even does it without notes. Some people claim to have a photographic memory; Andrew actually does. I've seen it in action many times, and it's one of the most impressive intellectual displays I've ever seen.

What you hold in your hands is a special narrative. I was riveted by every page, every word. Trust me: every Alabama fan will be captivated by this work—even the kids who are selling Cokes in the upper deck of Bryant-Denny Stadium.

>   —*Jay Barker* *was the starting quarterback on Alabama's 1992 national championship team. He currently hosts* The Jay Barker Show *on Tide 100.9 FM.*

CHAPTER 1

Lee Roy Jordan

The University of Alabama's storied program has produced many college football greats—Derrick Thomas, Cornelius Bennett, DeMeco Ryans, Jonathan Allen, and so on. But the best defensive player, arguably in both the Coach Paul W. Bryant era and the history of the program, is Lee Roy Jordan.

Jordan was a superstar on Coach Bryant's first national championship team at Alabama in 1961. He helped lead one of the most dominating defenses in the history of college football, which allowed just 2.3 points per game. Imagine only giving up 25 points in an entire season. The most points scored against the Crimson Tide in 1961 were seven by North Carolina State. Alabama blasted Auburn 34–0 and finished the season 11–0 after a win against Arkansas, who at the time was a member of the Southwest Conference. The Tide were crowned national champions prior to its bowl game against Arkansas, which was standard.

Freshmen were not eligible to play on a college varsity team for any sport until 1968 when the NCAA allowed participation in all sports except football and basketball. Freshmen became eligible to play in football and basketball in 1972–73. So Jordan began officially playing for the Crimson Tide during the 1960 season. He is remembered for his 31 tackles in 17–0 win against Oklahoma in the 1963 Orange Bowl. That was his final game as a player for Alabama, and it was also attended by president John F. Kennedy.

Jordan's story started long before his Hall of Fame career in Tuscaloosa and 14 years with the Dallas Cowboys. He recalled making his first tackle at 12 years old in 1953 and didn't stop putting ball carriers in the dirt until he retired after the 1976 season. The farm life turned Jordan into an All-American at Alabama, a five-time Pro Bowl selection, the NFL Defensive Player of the Year (1973), and Super Bowl champion (1971). But Jordan will never forget where he came from or the foundation set forth by his family.

Jordan was born on April 27, 1941, to Walter and Cleo Jordan, who were from south Alabama. He was part of a big family with three older brothers: Walter Jr., Carl, and Bennie Ray. He also had three sisters: Lottie, Agnes, and Darlene. The latter passed away at age 2 of leukemia. The family lived in a very small, rural farming community in Excel, Alabama, in Monroe County about 80 miles northeast of Mobile. The population was fewer than 350 in the 1940s and '50s, and fewer than 800 people lived in Excel as of 2018. He started working daily on his family's farm at only 4 years old at the end of World War II in 1945. "I was raised on a farm," Jordan said. "We raised everything you could eat. We raised our own beef, pork, vegetables. We really had one hell of a garden. My mother was an extremely good cook. I am still envious of her cooking ability to this day. It was a small town. We were out in the country. We actually didn't have electricity until I was 12 years old. It was very rural."

Jordan grew up riding on horses and wagons until he was 10 years old when his father bought a truck. Two years later the family purchased a radio. The Jordans also had a cotton field and grew peanuts. "We had a big family and we all had work to do," he said. "There were four boys and three girls. We knew what hard work was almost immediately. My mother and father introduced that to us right off the bat. They really taught us how to work and to be responsible."

There were not a lot of opportunities to play multiple sports in the early 1950s in his small town. There were no golf or tennis teams. There was not even a baseball team. Jordan had two options: football and basketball and he became an all-district basketball player. Jordan remembers the first time he made his first stop on the football field. "I was going to practice with my brothers, who were playing high school football," he said. "The coach [Al Brandon] asked me if I would stand back in the safety position on the defensive side of the ball so they knew someone would be back there. After about two or three days, I finally just came up and tackled one of the boys. I did it without a helmet. The coach wanted me to be a part of the team after that. I was 12 years old."

Jordan played on both sides of the ball throughout his high school career. He gives a lot of credit for his development to his head coach, W.C. Majors, and his assistant coach, Joe Weaver. Coach Majors and Coach Weaver remained close with Jordan for many years. Coach Bryant became the head coach at the University of Alabama in 1958, and Coach Majors attended coaching clinics in Tuscaloosa, where he learned all he could from Coach Bryant. Jordan hit a growth spurt (gained 30 pounds and grew three inches) prior to his junior season when Alabama started taking notice in his athletic abilities. "I played linebacker and running back throughout high school," Jordan said. "I loved being a linebacker. I loved hitting someone rather than being hit. The moment I realized I had an opportunity to possibly go to college to play football was during my junior season. We were playing W.S. Neal in Brewton, Alabama. Alabama assistant coach Jerry Claiborne was scouting another player from the other team. I had a better game than the other guy. He came over to the dressing room to introduce himself. He said he would be back next year, and they would be keeping up with me. That's when it all started for me."

Coach Bryant arrived at Alabama during Jordan's junior season in high school. The legendary coach from Moro Bottom, Arkansas, was a defensive end for Alabama from 1933 to 1935. He also worked as an assistant coach for the Tide between 1936–40. Coach Bryant received his first head coaching opportunity at the University of Maryland in 1945. He spent one season at Maryland before becoming the head coach at Kentucky. Bryant had led Kentucky to its first SEC championship in 1950 and finished with a top 20 team each of the next three seasons. Bryant resigned from Kentucky because the basketball program led by Adolph Rupp was considered the top sport in Lexington, Kentucky, and outshined football. Bryant then became the head coach at Texas A&M, where the "Junction Boys" training camp began prior to his first season in College Station, Texas.

Texas A&M finished the 1954 season 1–9. It was Coach Bryant's only losing season as a head football coach. Coach Bryant led the Aggies to the 1956 Southwest Conference championship with a 34–21 win against Texas. Meanwhile, Alabama had suffered back-to-back 2–7 seasons under head coach Ears Whitworth. His career record in Tuscaloosa was 4–24–2, which included a 14-game losing streak between 1955 and 1956. Alabama athletics director Hank Crisp flew to Houston to convince Coach Bryant to take the Alabama job, "Get your ass to Tuscaloosa where you belong so we can start winning football games," he said according to Allen Barra's book, *The Last Coach*. Coach Bryant announced on December 3,

1957 he would return to Alabama to become its head coach. When asked by reporters about returning to his alma mater, he said, "Mama called. And when Mama calls, you just have to come running."

Jordan knew there was a lot of excitement throughout Alabama when Coach Bryant returned to Tuscaloosa from talking to his high school coaches and listening to the radio.

A College Football Hall of Fame coach, Claiborne was an Alabama assistant with Bryant from 1958 to 1960 before becoming the head coach at Virginia Tech, and he was the first to take notice of Jordan's skills during his junior season. But Jordan said all that really mattered was Coach Bryant being the head coach at Alabama. "I was also recruited by Auburn and Southern Miss," he said. "A few other smaller schools recruited me. I visited Auburn, but when I heard Coach Bryant was coming home, my mind had already been made up that I wanted to play for him. I really didn't know much about being a college football fan in the 1950s. There wasn't all the exposure like there is now. You have to pick a side now, but back then I really didn't follow college football much. I was learning about the schools when I took the visits."

Auburn seemed like the most logical choice for Jordan because of his farming background. He expected to continue the family tradition after graduating from college. "It seemed like a natural fit for me because they were an agricultural school," he said. "I was impressed by that. I was thinking at the time I would come home and be a farmer. I thought I would get more experience at Auburn doing that than I would at Alabama, but once I met Coach Bryant, I was set on going to Alabama."

It was an easy decision for Jordan after meeting Coach Bryant. He was naturally a defensive-oriented coach after playing defensive end for

Alabama and remained partial to defensive players. It doesn't come as a surprise that Jordan was a perfect fit. "I remember meeting Coach Bryant in his office," Jordan said. "He had this desk that was up on a pedestal. He was looking down on you while you were sitting there in a chair. He invited me to come play for the University of Alabama. I think I accepted on about the third word he was able to get out of his mouth."

Jordan was officially a part of the 1959 recruiting class for Alabama. He was the first of his family to attend college. His three older brothers all joined the military after high school. Jordan played on both sides of the ball for the Crimson Tide as a linebacker and center at 6'1" and 210 pounds. He moved strictly to linebacker midway through his junior season when Coach Bryant put sophomore Gaylon McCollough, who eventually became a noted plastic surgeon, in at center.

Jordan was the MVP in the Bluebonnet Bowl against Texas during his sophomore season. He helped Alabama to the 1961 national championship, which included six shutouts. Alabama finished 10–1 during Jordan's senior season. The Crimson Tide lost 7–6 at Georgia Tech (a member of the SEC until 1964). It was Alabama's first loss in more than two years.

The Alabama defense gave up only 39 points in 1962. The Crimson Tide didn't win the national championship that year. USC, which was led by John McKay, finished the season 10–0, won its bowl game against Wisconsin, and was declared by polls as the national champion. Alabama played in the Orange Bowl against Oklahoma, in which President Kennedy attended. Jordan, an Alabama captain, took part in the ceremonial coin toss, which occurred in the stands rather than on the field because of security issues. Jordan called tails. He won the toss and received the commemorative coin, something he has kept to this day. Alabama may have felt slighted before kickoff as President Kennedy was on the Oklahoma side of the stadium, but it didn't matter to Jordan, who went on to have a legendary performance. He was credited with 31 tackles and was named MVP. It was his second time winning an MVP award in a bowl game during his career with the Crimson Tide.

Jordan was a unanimous All-American after his senior season and was named Lineman of the Year in college football. "He was one of the finest football players the world has ever seen," Bryant said, according to the National Football Foundation. "If runners stayed between the sidelines, he tackled them. He never had a bad day. He was 100 percent every day in practice and in the games."

Jordan and Coach Bryant were one in the same. They demanded perfection. They wanted everyone to give it their all on every play. It's what Jordan was known for throughout his career. "Playing for Coach Bryant was great," he said. "He loved hard work. He demanded that from everyone on the team. You had to go 100 percent on every play in practice as well as the game. He would call you out on it if you didn't. He would embarrass you in front of your teammates, and it would make you not want to disappoint him ever again."

In his autobiography, *Bear: The Hard Life and Good Times of Alabama's Coach Bryant,* Bryant raved about Jordan. "I never had another one like Lee Roy Jordan. He was a center/linebacker, going both ways at 190 pounds, playing against guys like Jackie Burkett of Auburn, who was 6'3", 235 pounds...It's a wonder I didn't foul him up because I tried him at two, three different positions as a sophomore, including offensive tackle, before he became a linebacker—the best linebacker in college football, bar none. He would have made every tackle on every play if they had stayed in bounds."

Following his senior season, Jordan was drafted sixth overall in the NFL draft by the Cowboys in 1963. He was also drafted 13th overall by the Boston Patriots of the AFL. Jordan played all 14 seasons with the Cowboys and started 173 games. Jordan was known as "killer" by his teammates in Dallas, where he amassed 1,236 tackles and 32 interceptions during his career. Jordan was a captain for the Cowboys' "Doomsday Defense" in the '60s and early '70s. He helped the Cowboys reach three Super Bowls and defeated the Miami Dolphins in 1972 for his first professional championship. "He was a great competitor," said NFL Hall of Fame head coach Tom Landry, according to dallascowboys.com. Landry coached the Cowboys for 29 seasons, including all 14 of Jordan's career. "He was not big for a middle linebacker, but because of his competitiveness, he was able to play the game and play it well. His leadership was there, and he demanded a lot out of the people around him as he did himself."

Jordan often returns to Tuscaloosa as he travels with his wife, Biddie, who he met in biology class at Alabama, to at least two home games each season. His passion for the Crimson Tide remains strong. "I love it," Jordan said. "I'm an Alabama boy and an Alabama supporter. I have loved everything that has gone on with the team under Coach Saban. It has been a very special thing to go back to Tuscaloosa as often as we can."

Jordan purchased the Redwood Lumber Company and renamed it The Lee Roy Jordan Redwood Lumber Company in 1977, and it is based in Dallas, Texas. Jordan and his wife have three sons: David, Lee, and Chris. He is a member of the Alabama Sports Hall of Fame, the College Football Hall of Fame, the Senior Bowl Hall of Fame, and was inducted into the Cowboys' Ring of Honor in 1990.

CHAPTER 2

David Palmer

The deuce is loose. One of the most spectacular football players in Alabama's storied program, David Palmer, who wore No. 2, finished third in the Heisman Trophy voting in 1993 behind Charlie Ward, who helped guide Florida State to its first ever national championship, and Tennessee quarterback Heath Shuler. Palmer could have been on the same team with Ward, but other factors, including wanting to be closer to his family and former FSU head coach Bobby Bowden telling him he would redshirt as a freshman, played a bigger role in his decision to stay in state. Palmer had three children in high school, which made going out of state a little more difficult.

He followed in the footsteps of former Alabama greats who grew up in Birmingham. "I watched a lot of high school football in town growing up," Palmer said. "Cornelius Bennett and Bobby Humphrey were the guys I looked up to. They both went to Alabama. Alabama was definitely a school I felt like I could get on the field early. I didn't want to be redshirted. Coach Stallings was also going to give me the opportunity to play baseball. I chose not to play baseball just because stuff happens so fast and I didn't want to get behind."

Palmer recognized his talent at an early age. The Birmingham native knew he always wanted to be in the spotlight. "I started playing football since I was 5 or 6 years old," he said. "I was pretty much always around football. I always played a lot of positions but mainly quarterback and running back during my peewee football years."

Palmer teamed up with Sam Shade in his final year of peewee football. It was the first time he lined up at a different position: wide receiver. Palmer knew he didn't have an issue catching the ball. Several years later in 1993, he became Alabama's first 1,000-yard receiver. Shade was the established running back on the peewee team, and the team had a quarterback. It wasn't a big deal for Palmer, who went on to score six touchdowns in the Shug-Bear Bowl Peewee Classic at Legion Field in a record-setting performance, which still stands. Palmer had previously won a few peewee championships, but it was the first one he won with Shade. The two ended up together at Alabama, where they won the national title in 1992.

Jackson-Olin High School did not have the same luck on the football field prior to Palmer's arrival in high school. The football program was in the dumps with consistent 1–9 seasons. "I always wanted to go to Jackson-Olin, even though I stayed on the other side of town. I was supposed to go to Parker High School, but I really wanted to see if I could help change the program at Jackson-Olin," Palmer said. "The first year we went 3–6, so we won more games than they had won before I got there. The second year we were 7–3 and went to the playoffs. We finished 7–3 my third year, and my final year, we went 10–1. I felt like I did what I set out to do, which was helping turn the program around. Jackson-Olin always had this one school, where they would go and get their quarterback from. One day the quarterback threw the ball over my head. When I went to get it, I threw it back instead of running it back in. The coach hollered at me. I thought he was mad at me because I threw the ball. He told me to go back and throw it again. I did, and then he said he had himself a new quarterback. I played quarterback every year of high school. I enjoyed it. It was a way to put the ball in my hands on every play. If the play broke down, then I could improvise and make something happen."

Palmer believed in himself before high school coaches and maybe even some college coaches. However, his longtime mentor, Maurice Ford, believed in him the most. Ford grew up in the same neighborhood as Palmer. He looked after him and became the father figure he needed in his life at the time. "I was a little older," Ford said. "I was in college. I think he was around 7 or 8 years old. I just took to him. I tried to show him the right things. I would call him my nephew. You saw one of us; you saw the other. I took him to athletic events, college games, high school games. I remember telling a high school coach when he was in the eighth grade that someone was coming along that would change the Jackson-Olin program. David was 5-foot-6, 130 pounds at the time. They said, 'you don't mean that little bitty boy?'…It was the same when he got to Alabama. They didn't think he would be able to do all the same things he did in high school. Once again, I said, 'be patient and you'll see.'"

Football was the way out of the neighborhood. Ford knew that, and it was a big reason why he kept Palmer away from any negative aspects in the community. "It was rough for someone his age to manage going to school, having three kids, playing football, and having everyone after him," his mentor said. "I would keep him away from everyone. I would tell him you aren't going to parties after football games. He went home. He didn't have a father around. He knew him, but he wasn't in his life. He didn't understand why he couldn't go to parties. People were fighting and doing all kinds of crazy stuff. He understands now, but he didn't understand back then why I wouldn't let him go."

Jackson-Olin head coach Earl Cheatham was one of the creators of the Wildcat offense. While playing in that offense, Palmer had 3,000 all-purpose yards as a senior quarterback and was named Mr. Football in the state of Alabama in 1990. "My first two years, we ran the option quite a lot," Palmer said. "We never really had a lot of schools recruiting Jackson-Olin other than places like Alabama A&M, Alabama State, Jacksonville State, and Grambling. I never wanted to go to those small schools."

College coaches first started taking notice of Palmer's athletic ability when he was a freshman. North Carolina State was the first school. Others quickly followed suit. Most schools weren't exactly sure which position he would play. Some recruited him to play quarterback, some saw him as a defensive back, and others wanted him just as an athlete. "At first, I really wanted to go to Florida State," Palmer said. "They passed the ball a lot. I also really liked the atmosphere.

"I was never really sure what some schools wanted me to play. I was pretty good at doing multiple things. I think Alabama really wanted me to play defensive back. They needed some defensive backs and asked me what I wanted to play. I had won Mr. Football and I don't think they wanted me to go out of state. I told them I wanted to play wide receiver. I think I let my own self down. It was going to be the first time I wasn't playing for a black coach. I let that intimidate me a little bit. I actually wanted to play wide receiver and defensive back. I think if I would have come back for my senior season [at Alabama] I was going to play both.

"Arkansas really wanted me to play quarterback. They recruited another player from my school, Vincent Davis, who ended up transferring to Hampton in Virginia. I really didn't want to play quarterback in college. I think I could have done it. I did it a few times at Alabama, but there is a lot of expectations and pressure to play quarterback, especially at a big program in the SEC. I think I would have faired out well, though. Arkansas ran the option, and I did that a little bit in high school."

Palmer took a recruiting visit to the University of Pittsburgh. He would have been in the same recruiting class as Pro Football Hall of Fame running back Curtis Martin if he opted to travel north, but the cold weather was a little too much. "Pitt invited me and Vincent up for a visit," Palmer said. "They really wanted him at the time. You know it never really snowed in Alabama. When we went up there, it was snowing. I knew I didn't want to play there. Of course, then I happened to get drafted later on by the Minnesota Vikings. I guess it got me prepared for that."

Jim Fuller, who played for Paul W. "Bear" Bryant and coached at Alabama from 1984 to 1996, was in charge of recruiting Palmer for the University of Alabama. "What a task that was," Fuller said. "Not sure I ever recruited anyone like that. It was just different. David was a tough one. Anyone who recruited David was never sure where he was going to go. Hell yes, he made us sweat. It was always: who am I here to see tonight? Was I visiting with David or his coaches? David was just a really quiet kid. He told us the night before Signing Day he was coming to Alabama. It was just a tough recruitment all the way through."

Palmer grew up in a rough part of town. Coach Fuller always made sure everybody knew why he was in the neighborhood. "At that time you better be careful where you parked your car," Fuller said with a laugh. "I never really had any problems where I went. I would say 99 percent of the time everyone knew where I was going. I would always stop by the service station and always mentioned I was going to see David more as a protective measure."

Florida State was a perennial powerhouse under Coach Bowden, who is also a Birmingham native. The Seminoles heavily recruited Palmer and wanted him to become a part of the program. "People in my neighborhood didn't want me to go to Alabama," Palmer said. "They wanted me to go to Florida State. At the same time, a lot of people thought I couldn't do the same things in college that I did in high school because of my size and stature. I had a chip on my shoulder. I had something to prove. Bobby Bowden was at Florida State. I had built a very good relationship with him. He was really the one recruiting me. He is a hometown guy. I heard all about him growing up. I knew about him at Samford. I wanted to be around someone like him. They were becoming a powerhouse at the time. I also thought I fit in pretty good with those colors. They also had their names on the back of their jerseys. Alabama didn't at the time. I took my recruiting visit down to Florida State. I walked into the locker room. There was a jersey with my name on the back of it. That was so exciting to me at the time. It was something I would never forget."

While weighing Florida State vs. Alabama, Palmer's mentor helped guide him throughout the recruiting process and became a big influence in his decision. "Coach Stallings and Coach Jim Fuller did a really good job in recruiting him," Ford said. "Someone was calling or checking in on him every day. Florida State was strongly in the picture. Coach Bowden did a great job. He wanted a Birmingham kid at Florida State. They were playing in a Pigskin Classic to open the season. They wanted David to return kicks for them in the game. Florida State was rolling back then. I knew it was hard for him to turn down. The whole recruiting process was hectic. It was the first time being in that situation. He didn't talk much, so he was referring everyone to talk to his uncle. So I was getting calls all the time asking if I had five minutes to speak."

The most persuasive figure might have been John "Big Daddy" Bishop. He founded Dreamland Bar-B-Que in 1958, and it originated in the Jerusalem Heights neighborhood in Tuscaloosa. The Alabama Crimson Tide football program has purchased countless racks of ribs for recruiting purposes. "I took my recruiting trip down to Alabama, and the first thing I asked is if they had a jersey with my name on the back of it," Palmer said. "They didn't, but they put me with five guys on the team who hosted me that weekend. I will say what really got me though was when they put those Dreamland ribs on you. Dreamland gets you every time. I bet those ribs got a lot of us back then."

Palmer got a lot of playing time in three different sports in high school. Along with football, he also starred in basketball and baseball. Alabama head coach Gene Stallings told him the opportunity was available to play baseball. "He was just a really, really good athlete," Fuller said. "We probably spent more time recruiting him in basketball than we did football. We just had a few visits for football. The football coaches recruited him as much as we could, but we always made sure someone was there. We'd leave the basketball games and drive by his house just to see which football coaches were visiting him that night."

In the end the football star went with his home team. "I got a chance to represent my whole team," he said. "It was a great opportunity for me. A lot of people didn't have the chance to go play football at Alabama. They weren't getting big-time scholarships. I could go down there and put on that crimson and white. I could make people proud. I grew up watching Alabama. When I was young, I would go watch Alabama play at Legion Field. That was my goal. That's what I did. I had three kids in high school. I would have put a big dent in my relationship with them if I would have gone to Florida State. Alabama was closer to them, so I chose Alabama. My momma was good with my decision. She was happy with the decision I made. I think back in the day with the segregation, tension, and just everything that had previously gone on, there were people in my community who didn't want me to go to Alabama. It was a decision I had to make. Who in Alabama doesn't want to play for Alabama? It's great tradition. They win. There wasn't a better decision for me. We won a national championship while I was there. We should have won three."

Alabama put names on the back of its jerseys when Palmer officially arrived in Tuscaloosa. He had to work some magic, though, on getting No. 2. Palmer was given No. 20 upon enrolling in Tuscaloosa, and someone else was given Palmer's famed jersey number. "I had always worn No. 2," Palmer said. "When I got to Alabama, they had given No. 2 to Dameian Jeffries. We were in the same class. We had battled for Mr. Football. I finished No. 1, and he finished No. 2. I think at the time Alabama wanted him more than they wanted me. They didn't know if he was going to play tight end or defensive line. He ended up playing on the defensive line. I told him if he would have stayed at tight end, he would have played a long time in the NFL."

Palmer and running back Sherman Williams, who was his Tide roommate and was assigned No. 44, went to talk to Jeffries (who was No. 2) about switching jerseys. So Jeffries took No. 44 (from Williams), Palmer got No. 2 (from Jeffries), and Williams took No. 20 (from Palmer). "Sherman and I had the idea to go talk to Dameian and switch jerseys," Palmer said. "We switched numbers without even telling the coaches. Sherman got my number. I got Dameian's. I'm just so glad they understood what it meant."

While playing with Williams, Palmer demonstrated his ability. "I remember meeting up with Sherman Williams at the Alabama/Mississippi All-Star Game. We planned on being roommates at Alabama and we were going to go down early to start practicing with the team. We wanted to get a head start. I get down to Alabama and I was doing one-on-ones. I was going up against future NFL first-rounder Antonio Langham and Mark McMillian, who was also drafted. They had grass shoes on, and I only had turf shoes. I was beating them. That helped my confidence out a lot. I knew I could play with them after beating them with my turf shoes."

Deuce, as he is widely known to Alabama fans across the country, played for Alabama from 1991 to 1993. He was one of the most electrifying playmakers to ever suit up for the Tide. He earned consensus first-team All-American honors after his junior season. His career stats included 102 receptions for 1,611 yards and 11 touchdowns. He had 86 rushing attempts and a touchdown. He also completed 15-of-20 passes for 260 yards and two touchdowns. He was regarded as one of the most dangerous return men in college football. He had 83 punt returns and four touchdowns. He also returned 36 kickoffs for 841 yards. Palmer decided to forego his senior season and enter the NFL draft. "There were just two of us with my momma growing up," he said, "my brother [Robert] and me. I think I was around 8 or 9 when my mom adopted two kids. Their parents just weren't around. My mom took them in. That's when things kind of changed for me. She instilled good values in us. Just watching her take care of us really laid a good foundation for the rest of my life."

Palmer played seven seasons in the NFL for the Vikings. He was primarily used as a kick returner and led the NFL in punt returns in 1995. He returned two punts and one kickoff for a touchdown. He also had one rushing and one receiving touchdown.

He currently resides in Birmingham, where he works at Hoover High School with Down syndrome and mentally challenged children. Palmer also started the Palmer Williams Group with Williams, his longtime teammate and friend. It provides programs to help disadvantaged youth to overcome obstacles.

CHAPTER 3

Johnny Musso

Rocky Balboa was nicknamed the "Italian Stallion." But prior to Sylvester Stallone's portrayal of the boxer from Philadelphia, which captured the Academy Award for Best Picture in 1977, there was an All-American who made the "Italian Stallion" nickname quite popular. Johnny Musso was a star football player for the University of Alabama. He grew up in the east part of Birmingham and was the epitome of grit and toughness throughout his playing days. The former University of Alabama trainer Jim Goostree is famous for saying, "He just chewed up opponents, wanted to kill them off with his running and blocking. He always gave total effort and he did it without regard to the punishment he was taking."

Musso was born on March 6, 1950. He is one of four children raised by a single mother, Josie, after his father passed away prior to his second birthday. "My dad died before I knew him," Musso said. "My mom raised the four of us. She is my hero. She is my hero in life. She still is. She has a space in my life that can't be filled besides the good Lord Jesus. I had three great siblings. I had an older sister, Mary Joe, who was like my mother. She filled both roles of acting as a mother because our mom worked a lot to provide for us. My sister went to Auburn for a few years. She was really an important and loving person in my life. My brothers and I started pulling for Alabama probably just to irritate her."

Paul W. "Bear" Bryant returned to Alabama in 1958. There was a lot of excitement throughout the state about his return to his alma mater. Musso listened to the radio broadcasts of Alabama games like a lot of Crimson Tide fans did in those days. It wasn't Coach Bryant, though, who captivated Musso's attention. It was an All-American linebacker. "Coach Bryant came to Alabama when I was around 8 or 9 years old," Musso said. "Alabama started to compete, and there was a lot of enthusiasm for the team. I really started to become an Alabama fan. My earliest memory on deciding on which school to pull for is during the Lee Roy Jordan era when Alabama competed for a national championship in '61. I got an invite from my cousin to go see Alabama play Auburn in the Iron Bowl. I thought he was giving me a ticket to go to the game, but that wasn't true.

"We met at the bus station and rode it to Legion Field. My older brother, my older cousin, and younger cousin were with me. Apparently, my cousins had snuck into the stadium before. I found out on the way to the stadium we were going to sneak in. We got there early because that was the best time to sneak into the stadium. I think the people, who were working the gate, were on to them immediately. My older cousin and brother got in. There was a barb-wire fence. My brother's sweater was caught on it. He wiggled out of it and was able to drop down. They got inside the stadium and ran. They left me and my younger cousin. I was only about 10 years old at the time. I didn't even really know how we got to the stadium. My cousins had done it before. They got in a time or two. My cousin was standing there. He said, 'I'm going to go for it.' I said, 'what?'

Then he ran through the railing that looks just look a long chute. It was about six feet long with an iron bar on each side. It was early, but there wasn't much activity going on, and the ticket takers weren't paying much attention. He gets through and runs up the ramp. When he got far enough up and realized nobody was following him, he yells down at me, 'Johnny come on!'

"I looked at the ticket takers. They were looking up at him, so I made a run for it. I ran by the ticket takers, and one tried to grab me. That's the moment I broke my first tackle. I ran up the ramp, and then we ran into the stadium. I remember we ran down the tunnel under the stadium to the seating area. It was kind of dark under the stadium, but then we walked out, and it was a perfect fall afternoon. Football was in the air. The excitement, the noise, the colors, it was my first experience at a college football game. It was the 1961 Iron Bowl, which Alabama won and went on to win the national championship. I remember we saw Coach Bryant get off the bus and go in the locker room. That was cool and all, but it was nothing compared to seeing Lee Roy Jordan get off the bus. We used to listen to the games on the radio. They would describe Lee Roy running side to side and ripping people's heads off. They were describing him in ways that our imagination went into overdrive. Just to see Lee Roy Jordan was a real thrill. He was my hero. We went home on the bus that day after Alabama's win against Auburn, and I remember all the excitement from the fans. It was just a great day and great experience for me. I think my allegiance to Alabama was solidified on that day."

Musso may have considered himself born to run after his first Iron Bowl experience, but it wasn't until a coach nicknamed Papa Rick started teaching him how to play football that the Italian Stallion was born. "I started playing baseball when I was 8 years old," Musso said.

"The baseball coach also coached football and he asked me to come out to play. I was 10 years old and started playing YMCA ball. I was always a running back. I got some of the best coaching from a man named Papa Rick, Mr. Rickles, but we called him "Papa Rick." He had these old gnarly fingers. He was giving me all of his years of experience. He gave me the football and pointed to the end zone. He said, 'now you run yan way, buddy, buddy. Just run yan way.' I guess that's as good of advice as I ever got."

A few years after Alabama High School Sports Hall of Fame coach George "Shorty" White became the head coach at Banks High School in Birmingham, a young Musso caught his attention during the freshmen team practice. Musso was glad he did not get discouraged prior to the start of the year because of his size or lack thereof. "I remember sitting in the bleachers," he said. "Banks had a lot of excitement around its athletic programs at the time. A lot of people were participating. A lot of folks were out there that day. This guy stood up, a coach, he said if you weigh less than 130 pounds, raise your hand. I raised my hand along with a few others. He said, 'I think you should consider playing YMCA one more year. They have a YMCA league if you are 130 pounds or less. You can play even if you are beyond age.' He said, 'You might have a better experience there.' I still went out for the high school team like most others did. The only thing I remember about my freshman year is Coach 'Shorty' White walking up beside me. I was playing defensive back on the freshmen team. He walked up and over my shoulder; he started coaching me. The varsity team had ended its practice... He gave me some pointers. Anytime I saw him around he knew my name. He would wave or something. There was a connection all of a sudden with the head coach."

Coach White may not have known it at the time, but he was grooming Musso to become his star athlete on his championship season the following year in 1965. Sophomores seldom played at Banks High School in the 1960s. Musso assumed he was on B team rather than the A team because of his size. But White encouraged him on how to gain weight and potentially make the A squad the following season. He started working out every day—some days with his head coach. Musso gained 35 pounds and was up to 165 pounds by the start of his sophomore season.

Musso joined Phil Cochran (who later signed with Auburn) as the only two sophomores on the varsity team in the fall. He had listened to Coach White a year prior on the practice field and was placed in the same position. It wasn't until late in the season when starting running back, Johnny Johnston, went down with an injury that he had the opportunity to showcase his skills in the offensive backfield. "I started as a cornerback during my sophomore season, and we won the state championship," Musso said. "It was the most fun I've ever had. It was a magical year. I was just a sophomore. A couple of seniors really took me under their wing. They let me run around with them. I was in awe of them. They became friends of mine and still are to this day."

Banks High School versus Woodlawn High School was *the* football rivalry in Birmingham during the time period. It was as intense as Alabama vs. Auburn. Just ask the 42,000 fans who attended the rivalry game in 1974, which is known as the biggest high school game in the history of the state. Nine years prior, Musso was creating his own legacy in the rivalry game and still has a souvenir to this day. "The game that definitely sticks out to me—and one I will always remember—is our game against Woodlawn when I was a sophomore," he said. "It was a big game. Both of us were undefeated. I scored the go-ahead touchdown in the fourth quarter. It was the greatest thrill of my life at that time. It's still pretty high up there, definitely memorable. I went into the corner of the end zone at Legion Field. It was my first ever touchdown and it mattered. I had been starting for three or four games at running back, but I hadn't scored yet. This was my first one. The game ended on that score. They had a chance to win in the end. They had a wide-open guy in the end zone, but our defensive back knocked the ball down. We won the game. I grabbed some grass and pulled it out of the turf. I put it in my sock. I still have that piece of grass today."

It may have been Musso's game against Woodlawn as a sophomore or perhaps the following season, when he had 1,000 yards rushing in 10 games, when he started receiving interest from Alabama and Auburn. Other top programs such as Florida, Georgia, and Tennessee were also coming after him. "Banks turned out a lot of really good D-I athletes back then," he said. "Other than Alabama and Auburn, I seriously considered Tennessee and Georgia. I decided fairly quickly in the process it was going to be Alabama or Auburn. I did visit those other schools. First, it was fun, and you wanted to see other programs. They were enjoyable, but it came down to Alabama and Auburn."

Musso did not see Auburn beat Alabama during his high school days, but he knew the Tigers were building its program. He remembers Auburn having a better recruiting class than Alabama in 1967, and the class in 1968 was led by future Heisman Trophy winner, Pat Sullivan. "Auburn was getting a lot of good players from outside the city of Birmingham and even some within like Pat Sullivan," Musso said. "I became very good friends with Pat and remained friends. Our friendship deepened as we competed against each other. I had to get real serious about it. It was very hard at the time because Auburn was rejuvenating its program. They had out-recruited Alabama the year before. They were recruiting really hard when I was a senior. Pat had already committed. Scott Hunter was at Alabama. Pat knew pretty early he was going to Auburn. He and I were the top two players in the state. I think a lot of guys went Auburn's way once Pat committed. I was really uncertain on the right place for me to go. It was the hardest decision I ever had to make. You made friends with people from Alabama and Auburn. I built caring relationships on both sides. Having to tell one coach I wasn't coming to their school was really hard to do. I don't remember a decision that was hard or had more ramifications on my life besides my relationship with the Lord Jesus."

Sam Bailey, the former Alabama running back coach, spent three decades serving various roles at Alabama. He was one of the coaches Musso built a strong connection to during his recruitment. The Alabama track and field complex is also named after Bailey. But it was Musso's older brother, Butch, who may have given him the key words that impacted his college decision. "I didn't have a father growing up," Musso stated. "My brother was six years older than me. He was the father figure in my life. He was my big brother but a father figure. I remember him giving me some advice, and it really cleared the picture for me. I don't remember his exact words, but he said if I went to Auburn and things didn't work out, I would always question it and second-guess myself. If I go to Alabama, it's where I always wanted to go and it's always been in my heart. He said I can live with the consequence of your choice if I go to Alabama. It's really what I wanted all along. I think it was the right advice. We did struggle my first few years at Alabama against Auburn. I went to where my heart told me though. I think I made the right decision. Pat and I started our friendship in the recruiting process. We didn't play together, but I think we both chose the right place for each other. I've never looked back."

Alabama was the eventual choice for Musso, who took his recruitment late into his senior year. Coach Bryant recruiting Musso wasn't anything special for the top running back in the state. He was accustomed to Shug Jordan spending an exuberant amount of time recruiting him. Coach Bryant did not become a key figure, at least from a recruiting perspective, until late in the process when Musso considered himself an Auburn lean.

Musso had a meaningful conversation with Coach Bryant after an in-home visit. Johnny's mother had a home-cooked meal prepared for Coach Bryant's visit, which included extended family members. Musso and Bryant were able to have their very open, candid conversation with each other at Butch's apartment after dinner. The hour-long discussion changed Musso's life—and possibly Coach Bryant's as well. "I really got to peek into who Coach Bryant was that night," Musso said. "I was thinking I was going to Auburn. Coach Bryant is a very intimidating person. I don't think people talked to him very frankly. I think I was probably overly cocky. I said some things pretty frank to him. I told him how I thought Auburn had a better recruiting class and had a better one the year before. I think I got him a little fired up. I was just saying some of those things because I thought I was going to Auburn. I look back on it now and I really cherish our conversation. I saw the real man when we had our talk together.

"Alabama had been a passing team. They really weren't running the ball that much…I really didn't want to have 10 or less carries.

I had this fire burning in my gut that I wanted to be a really good player in college. Coach Bryant challenged me and said I would get the opportunity to be a featured back. He would give me the opportunity if I proved myself. I got to see Coach Bryant's heart that night, and he saw mine. I think from that point on he treated me differently because he knew I didn't want to just be an average player. He did everything he said he was going to do. He gave me the opportunity and chance to prove myself."

Auburn came in second for Musso's signature, but it wasn't out of lack of respect for the program or the relationships he built with coaches or future All-Americans. Alabama was his first love. Coach Bryant challenged him and opened the door for him to thrive in Tuscaloosa. "I respect Auburn," he said. "I had such a good experience getting recruited by them. I made a lot of friendships during the recruiting process. There were a lot of guys who we were friends with who played for Auburn. It was a good, hard rivalry. Somewhere along the lines, it bottomed out. It turned mean and hateful at one point, but back when I was playing, it was like Banks and Woodlawn. It was a healthy rivalry. You fought hard and wanted to win. It meant a lot. It was always a respectful thing. I had grown up an Alabama fan. I was really pulling for them ever since I was young. The recruiting process is tough. You build a lot of relationships with players and coaches. I was just trying to figure out the right place for me. I was trying to choose between Alabama and Auburn. It was confusing. You have a lot of people throughout the recruiting process who you really care about. You aren't only trying to find the best place for you but also have to tell others, who recruited you for so long and built relationships with, that you are not going to their school. It's a tough process."

Musso strongly believes Alabama was the right decision. Did he question it at times during the early part of his career in Tuscaloosa? Absolutely. But more than 50 years later, he recognizes the impact his enrollment in Alabama had upon his life. "I would definitely say it was one of the most meaningful decisions of my life," he said. "Choosing to go to Alabama and the point in my life where I came to trust Jesus with my heart really made the most difference. The decision to go to Alabama really set that in motion as well. The younger you are when you make an important life decision, it will last with you longer. It's one of the most important decisions I ever made—from friends to the experiences I had. Those experiences served greater value than football. You learn a lot of life lessons and you build your character. I remember we were all glad to get it over with. It was much relief. I still didn't know if I made the right decision at the time. I think I made it for the right reasons. There were a lot of times in my head when I just wanted to follow other recruits [to Auburn], but I followed my heart. That's what I really wanted to do.

"There were plenty of times I second-guessed it. I got to Alabama and I had some opinions of myself. I knew I was the best running back in the state. I knew I was the best running back they signed. I didn't have any perspective. I remember watching a TV special. They did a spotlight on two recruits in the entire nation. One of the players was a running back named Jesse Causey, and he was going to Alabama. I'm thinking Alabama had their recruiting class revolving around me, and I find out I was just an add-on. When I was a freshman, they put me on defense, and they had Jesse on offense at running back."

Causey was one of the top running backs in the country and he hailed from Central High School in Miami. The high school

All-American transferred from Alabama after his freshman season. He suffered severed tendons and nerve damage after running through a glass door, which required nearly 500 stitches, and transferred to the University of Tampa.

Instead of Causey, Musso was the illustrious figure in the backfield from 1969 to 1971. He had 837 all-purpose yards and 13 touchdowns during his sophomore season. He rushed for 1,137 yards with nine touchdowns as a junior. In Musso's senior year, Alabama surprised the nation by opening the season in a wishbone offense. His year-end campaign totaled 1,088 yards and 16 touchdowns. He led the conference in rushing during his junior and senior seasons. He also led the SEC conference in scoring (100 points). Musso finished fourth in the Heisman Trophy voting after the 1971 season and was named Player of the Year by Football News, the Miami Touchdown Club, and Touchdown Club of Atlanta. He was also a two-time All-American and consensus All-American in 1971. Musso finished his career at the University of Alabama with 2,741 yards rushing and a school record 34 rushing touchdowns (a mark held until Shaun Alexander broke it in 1999). He was named All-SEC in 1970 and 1971.

Musso was a third-round selection in the 1972 NFL Draft by the Chicago Bears, but he signed with the British Colombia Lions of the Canadian Football League instead because it was a more lucrative offer. He also played one season for the Birmingham Vulcans in the World Football League before signing a contract with the Bears in 1975. He backed up Walter Payton before officially retiring from football in 1979. He is a member of the College Football Hall of Fame (2000) and the Alabama Sports Hall of Fame.

Musso entered the business world after his football career ended. He was president of a commodities firm called the Schreiner-Musso Trading

Company. He also served in youth ministry. Musso and his wife, Tanner, have five children (from oldest to youngest): Zach, Brian, Scott, Brad, and their only daughter, Tyler. Zach and Tyler followed in their father's footsteps by enrolling at the University of Alabama.

CHAPTER 4

John Hannah

In August 4, 1981, *Sports Illustrated* had John Hannah on its cover with the headline "The Best Offensive Lineman of All Time." The 6'2", 265 pounder was described as having the same lateral quickness as an NFL defensive back—just 80 pounds heavier. That is why perhaps the greatest offensive guard to ever play in the NFL earned All-Pro status in 10 straight seasons.

Hannah could have ended up playing for Clemson if it hadn't been for Hank Crisp, who spent many years at Alabama coaching various sports including basketball, baseball, and track. He also coached the line on the Alabama football team for several years. Crisp served as the Alabama athletic director from 1930 to 1940 and 1954 to 1957. The final order of business was hiring Paul W. "Bear" Bryant to return home to coach the Crimson Tide and become the athletic director.

The Clemson vs. Alabama decision also came to whether they could guarantee the best room and board. "My father, Herb Hannah, was in the Navy," John Hannah said. "He grew up during a pretty rough period in the Great Depression. World War II broke out, and he signed up immediately. He went to officer candidate school to become a pilot. He befriended a guy named Rock McCants from South Carolina. He kind of built his confidence up enough and said, 'Herb, you are going to go to college.' Dad said, 'okay, where am I going?' Rock was from Orangeburg, South Carolina, so he said Clemson. Dad had a half [veteran's] scholarship. He told the football coaches if they gave him half a football scholarship, a place to live, and three meals a day he would come to Clemson. They said, 'Herb, we can give you a half scholarship and a place to live, but we can only feed you two meals a day.' Dad had played football in the military for Hank Crisp. He goes down to Alabama to see Hank. He asked Hank for everything he asked Clemson. Hank says, 'Sure, Herb, we can do all that for you.' So, that's how dad ended up at Alabama."

Herb joined the Crimson Tide in 1947 as a 26-year old freshman. He played four seasons in Tuscaloosa and one season in the NFL with the New York Giants. He moved to Canton, Georgia, with his wife, Geneva, and on April 4, 1951, had their first son, John. He was raised in Canton until he was 6 years old. He spent one year in Alabama before moving back to Georgia. His family finally settled down in Albertville, Alabama, right before John entered the sixth grade.

His father originally worked on his father-in-law's dairy farm after his football days came to an end. His parents also worked as teachers, but by the time their third son, David, was born, they had retired from teaching and moved to Albertville. Herb worked in the agricultural business and founded the Hannah Supply Company in 1961, which built chicken houses and was a wholesale distributor for veterinary supplies.

John was a little pudgier than his friends at a young age. Football wasn't an escape for him until his father talked a coach into letting him play against older kids instead of getting called names by other kids his own age. "I started playing organized football when I was in the fourth grade," Hannah said. "I was out on the field with my so-called friends. They kept calling me 'fatty, fatty, 2x4 can't fit through the kitchen door.' They were making fun of me. My mom found out about it, and she called my dad. He had coached some of the guys, who were coaching the sixth, seventh, and eighth grade team. He asked the coach if I could come up and play with them. He said, 'I think he can play with them. Do you mind if he comes out there?'...My dad came to me that night. He said, 'I have a way. It's not gonna be easy. It's gonna be hard, but I have a way for you to never be called 'fatty, fatty, 2x4 again.'"

John Hannah ended up starting for them, and that's how football came into his life.

Hannah then attended Baylor School in Chattanooga, Tennessee, from his freshman year until he was a senior. He excelled in football, of course, but was also an outstanding wrestler and still holds the Baylor record in discus and shot put in track and field. He gives a lot of credit to major Luke Worsham, whom he thanked in the beginning of his acceptance speech to the Pro Football Hall of Fame.

Worsham coached Hannah on the offensive line during his three years at Baylor School and also talked him into coming out for the wrestling team during his ninth grade year. The World War II veteran was inducted into the Tennessee Sports Hall of Fame in 2006, and the wrestling facility at Baylor School is named in his honor. Hannah was a national champion in wrestling in 1967. He moved home and attended Albertville High School in Alabama during his senior year.

College coaches were well aware of the kid nicknamed "Hog" and knew he was going to play college football. His father and his Uncle Bill played for the Crimson Tide. Former Alabama quarterback Steve

Sloan was an assistant coach for Alabama between from 1968 to 1970. He first noticed Hannah during his junior season at Baylor. Alabama started showing increased interest after that, and soon others began to follow.

It was rare for juniors to attract recruiting attention in the late 1960s. It typically wasn't until a recruit's senior season when scholarship offers were extended. Hannah was a heavily recruited player during his senior year, but his mind was pretty much made up when his dad, the man who wanted three meals a day to go to Alabama, told him what it would be like when he came home from college if he chose another school. "My first official offer came some time during my senior season," Hannah said. "The University of Georgia was heavily recruiting me. Back then nobody was offered until their senior season. Tennessee wanted me to come see them. My Uncle Bill was actually coaching at Cal-State Fullerton at the time of my recruitment. He found out I may consider someplace else besides Alabama. So he had Southern Cal start recruiting me. I narrowed it down to three schools: Alabama, Georgia, and Southern Cal. One day I came home. My dad said, 'Have you decided yet?' I said no. He said, 'John, I'll root for you wherever you decide to go. I'll come visit you and watch you play. The thing you have to worry about is where you're gonna eat when you come home.' That pretty much decided where I was going to go."

The visit to Alabama was different than others. There was a simple recruiting pitch by the six-time national champion head coach, who had captured three championships prior to Hannah's arrival. Bryant took a different approach to recruiting the youngest brother, David, who was recruited and signed by Alabama in 1975. Bryant also recruited and signed his middle brother, Charley, in

1973. Charley played 12 seasons in the NFL and won a Super Bowl with the Los Angeles Raiders in 1984. "We went down for our visit," John Hannah stated. "They called us in the alumni room in the old coliseum. Coach Bryant basically said, 'Welcome. We have to go get ready for a game. I just want to say one thing: if you want to win a national championship, this is the place to do it, and it's the only place to do it.' Then he left. That was it. I didn't get a whole lot of push from him. It was basically just come or don't come. That was all he did. We are going to be national champs; you can either join us or don't.

"I had the closest relationship during the recruitment with Steve Sloan. I didn't really get recruited by Coach Bryant other than the time I went down to Alabama for my visit, and he gave the speech to all of us about coming to Alabama to be national champions. Both of my brothers were recruited by Coach Bryant probably more heavily than me, especially David. Coach Bryant never really recruited me, but he came to my house to sign David. David could have been the best of all of us if he didn't get hurt so bad. He was just a naturally born offensive lineman. The reason I chose Alabama was primarily because of the family heritage. My dad and uncle had gone there. Even though I was thinking about other schools, there was really no doubt about where I was going to go."

Hannah played tackle and guard during his time in Tuscaloosa from 1970 to 1972. In fact, Hannah was the heaviest player Bryant had recruited at 265 pounds. He was a two-time All-American. He helped the Crimson Tide to an SEC championship in 1971 and 1972. Alabama didn't climb to the mountain top and win a national championship during Hannah's time in Tuscaloosa. But Alabama won the national championship in 1973, the year after Hannah moved on to the NFL. Hannah was a three-sport star at Alabama. He was an SEC champion wrestler and was the SEC record holder for a long time in the shot put and discus. He also won the SEC Jacobs Trophy given to the best blocker in the conference and finished 11th in Heisman voting during his senior year. That's amazing to think an offensive lineman could receive Heisman votes. Hannah was described by Coach Bryant as the "best offensive lineman I ever coached."

Hannah was drafted No. 4 overall in the 1973 NFL Draft by the New England Patriots. He played 13 seasons with the Patriots and had nine Pro Bowl berths. He was also named All-Pro 10 straight years (1976–1986). He earned the NFL Players' Association Offensive Lineman of the Year honors four straight years (1978–1981). He was the power driver in the offensive line, which helped set an NFL record with 3,165 rushing yards. That mark stood until the Baltimore Ravens broke it during the 2019 season.

He was inducted into the NFL Hall of Fame in 1991 and the College Football Hall of Fame in 1999. He was inducted into the Alabama Sports Hall of Fame in 1988. He was the first player inducted in the Patriots Hall of Fame. Hannah retired after the Patriots lost to the Chicago Bears in Super Bowl XX in 1986. He was announced on the NFL All-Time 100 team by the NFL Network at Super Bowl LIV on February 2, 2020. Nowadays, Hannah resides on a farm between Arab and Blountsville in Alabama raising cattle.

His father, Herb, died in 2007, two years after his mom passed away. Hannah's father had the honor of introducing his son in the Pro Football Hall of Fame. His life must have flashed before his eyes from his friend, McCants, talking him into going to college to play football, to becoming a dairy farmer, moving to Albertville, and sending his sons to Baylor. Herb loved football and so did his brother and sons, who all played for the Crimson Tide. "When John was born, God gave him all the attributes of a great offensive guard," his father stated at Hannah's Pro Football Hall of Fame enshrinement in 1991. "He had the intelligence, physical talents, a winning attitude, a friendly desire for excellence, a competitive nature, and an unusual tolerance for pain. I, like the many fans who enjoyed watching John play, will always remember his exploding into a linebacker or a defensive lineman, leading the back off tackle, around end, or dropping back on pass protection, always giving it 100 percent on each and every play. The intensity of his play was always by the rules of the game and without any fanfare. He just went about doing his job Sunday after Sunday as good as or better than any offensive lineman that I ever saw play the game."

CHAPTER 5

Dwight Stephenson

Dwight Stephenson was the starting center for the University of Alabama from 1977 to 1979, and Alabama won back-to-back national championships in 1978 and 1979. Stephenson is one of the most decorated Alabama football players in history. He is a member of the Pro Football Hall of Fame and one of only four centers named to the NFL 100 all-time team. Despite all of those accolades, you wouldn't hear any talk of it from the source himself. "He didn't say very much, but he didn't have to," Paul W. "Bear" Bryant said.

Stephenson was just a kid from Murfreesboro, North Carolina, who grew up in Hampton, Virginia, and never expected his life to go in the direction of playing football for two legendary football coaches such as Coach Bryant at Alabama and Don Shula with the Miami Dolphins.

Instead he became a five-time Pro Bowler, first-team All-Pro in five consecutive seasons (1983–1987), NFL All-Decade Teamer in the 1980s, the NFL Man of the Year in 1985, Virginia Sports Hall of Famer, Walter Camp Man of the Year in 2005, and earned the Pro Football Focus' annual Dwight Stephenson Award given to the best overall player in the NFL regardless of position.

Stephenson was born in 1957 to Eugene Stephenson and Louise Brunson. His father grew up on a farm and decided to try his best at farming. "Both of my parents were from Murfreesboro," Dwight Stephenson said. "They only had about 2,500 people—if that—in the town. It was a big farming community. When they got married, my mother was 18, and my father was 19. They got married and started a family. I couldn't have asked for better parents. I had two of the best parents and family anyone could ask for."

Stephenson was the second of seven children. His sister, Joyce, was two years older. The leader of the Stephenson children, who was the first to go to college and set the standard for her siblings, Joyce passed away at the young age of 42 due to breast cancer in 1997.

Dwight Stephenson was 5 years old when the Stephensons moved to Virginia. His father started working as a mechanic for the Newport News Shipyard, which is the largest industrial employer in Virginia. "My mother and father come from real strong work ethic backgrounds," he said. "All they did growing up is work on the farm. My mother and father then raised seven kids. I don't think I ever saw my mom sit down. She was ready to go to bed when she got finished taking care of her kids every night. When I grew up, I thought everyone's father had two jobs. I would go a whole week without seeing my dad. He would work until five at the shipyard and then go to another job from five until midnight. He would work overtime on the weekends 90 percent of the time. I would get to see him some of Saturday night and on Sunday. I think everyone kind of followed that pattern of going to work in our family."

The parents wanted their children to have opportunities not available to them. That's why his father worked two jobs and his mother worked in the school cafeteria. "My father was a pretty decent athlete growing up," Stephenson said. "He didn't have the opportunity to play sports. I think he was working and finished school in the ninth grade. He always wanted his kids to be able to go to college. He made a way for all of that to happen. It was also always important to my mother for us to go off to school."

Stephenson's siblings included his oldest sister, Joyce; sister, Toni; followed by his brother, Michael; sister Tammie; sister Stephanie; and the youngest, Chris. His family enjoyed sports, but Chris was the only other one to play a sport at the next level. He went to St. Paul's College in Lawrenceville, Virginia. Both of his brothers also served in the military. Michael carried on his father's legacy by working at the same shipyard. His mother still remains in Hampton after Dwight's father passed away on January 2, 2007 to mesothelioma. "We were a close family," Stephenson said. "There were seven kids. We understand the team concept. We were always supporting each other. We all worked once we got to fifth grade—whether it was babysitting, cutting grass, or working in the store up the street. We worked and played sports. Tammie was a cheerleader. Joyce played basketball and was on the pep squad. Toni didn't play sports. Mike never played but loved sports. Chris, of course, played in college. Stephanie never played any sports. We were always supportive of each other."

Dwight's mother had to manage her time between working and raising her children and she praised him for taking a leading role in the house at a young age. "I had seven of them: four girls and three boys," Louise Stephenson said. "Dwight got a job when he was 10 or 12 years old and really helped look out for his brothers and sisters. I didn't want a lot of candy in the house, but he would always be slipping them some. He was always a good person. He was always looking out for them. I knew he liked playing basketball. I didn't go to many of his team events. I was working and had other children. His dad would always try to go see him. I went to a couple of games but not many."

Dwight credits his best friend, Kenny Gilliam, for encouraging him to play football along with former Hampton head coach Mike Smith. Both were in attendance for his Pro Football Hall of Fame induction in 1998. But Dwight was more of a basketball player until the 11th grade. "Basketball is what I really loved and wanted to play," he said. "I would go over to our recreational center, which was only half a mile from the house. I would go there every day. It was open every evening. I couldn't wait to play with the bigger guys. I always thought we had the greatest athletes in the world. I thought they were better than Julius Erving. Of course, they weren't, but that's what I thought at the time. I played on the junior high school basketball team and then played on the varsity team in 10th grade.

"Our varsity football coach, Mike Smith, wanted me to come out for football. I said 'yes, okay.' When the time came during the summer to go out, I really didn't know if I could play. I worked out with my best friend, Kenny Gilliam. He said, 'If I can do it, you can do it.' He was a superstar to me. He was telling me that he believed I could play, but then there were some who didn't think I was good enough. I just knew I wasn't going to quit. I think the first time I went out there, I got sick and started throwing up, but the next day, I was fine. I learned the game and, before I knew it, I was starting."

One of the best to ever play the game at center didn't start for his high school team at that position until his senior season. "I was starting on defense," Stephenson said, "And I was the backup center. The guy who was starting at center was leaving the next year, so I thought that might be my chance to get on offense."

Hampton High School had a great football tradition. It had won four state championships prior to Stephenson's arrival. The team lost to the eventual champion in 1974 during his junior season, but Stephenson's team came back victorious and knocked them off in 1975. "We were undefeated and we lost to the state champion, which was also our crosstown rival, Bethel High School. Coach told me when I was on defense that I had the pitch man and not to go after the fullback. The quarterback put the ball in that fullback's stomach, and I went after him. The quarterback pulled it back and he went for about 60 yards around me. I was like, *oh my goodness, that play just cost us the game.* It was a real learning experience for me. I was not going to make the same mistakes again. We were a good football team and we had a lot of talent coming back. I think we had seven or eight shutouts the next year. We beat our rival and went into the state championship game against Annandale High School. Things went our way that night, and we won."

Instead of Stephenson, defensive back Woodrow Wilson and defensive tackle Simon Gupton were the ones on his team receiving attention from colleges and they both signed with North Carolina State. "I wasn't the one receiving all the recruiting attention on my team," Stephenson said. "Those two guys could have gone anywhere in the country. Nobody was really talking to me. We were going to different places to visit: Temple, Virginia Tech, Clemson, East Carolina. All the coaches were really talking to Woodrow and Simon. I kind of said the first coach that calls and offers me a scholarship is where I am going. I am going to really appreciate that and go to that school. Well, Pat Dye was the coach at East Carolina and he was the first one to offer me. I came to the school the next morning and my coach, Coach Smith, meets me in the hallway. He always had a funny walk, like he owned the school. He said, 'The coach from East Carolina told me you are signing with them.' I told him, 'Well, Coach, they are the only school interested in me.' He told me to take my visits. So, I took visits to East Carolina and Virginia Tech. I think we visited Clemson, and Coach picked us up from the airport. He said, 'How would y'all like to go down to Alabama?' I think one of my teammates said, 'Where is that? Is that in Georgia?' We just said, 'Yeah, let's go.' We went down there, and they offered the two guys and said they were interested in me, too."

Stephenson knew after the trip to the University of Alabama it was possibly the best spot for him, but he still didn't know if he wanted to go that far from home. He had five younger siblings. His parents were constantly working, and it would be difficult for them to travel often to see him play. North Carolina State was less than 200 miles away while Tuscaloosa was close to 800 miles from home. "I didn't want him to go that far," his mother said. "His dad always watched football. He knew Alabama was a good school. Before I left the house one night to go pick up his dad, Dwight asked me, 'Mom, what do you think I should do?' I told him it was his decision and not to let me or his dad influence him. His dad wanted him to go to Alabama. I didn't want him to go. When I went to pick up his dad, I was crying the whole way. He signed with Alabama. I think he made a really good decision, but at the time, I really didn't want him to go that far."

His mother may not have wanted him to go far from home, but she also wanted him to venture out on his own and carve his own legacy rather than following in the footsteps of his teammates. "I had it in my mind that I was going to Alabama, but at the same time, I was a little intimidated going down there by myself," Dwight said. "So I thought about going to N.C. State, but my mother said I wasn't going there. I wasn't going to go follow someone else. That decided that."

Ken Donahue and John Mitchell were the Alabama coaches in charge of recruiting Stephenson to Alabama. Mitchell, along with Wilbur Jackson, were the first African American football players to play at the University of Alabama. Dwight's mother remembers the coaches coming to the house. She spent most of the time listening to the conversations and seeing how her son felt comfortable with the coaches who were wanting him to come play for the Crimson Tide. "Coach Donahue was like Abraham Lincoln," Dwight said. "He was tall, thin, with a narrow face. Coach Donahue was really the heartbeat of the team. He pushed everybody. It was amazing to be around him. Coach Mitchell was a class guy. He set a very good example for me. They were both just great people and great coaches. I am thankful for them getting me to Alabama."

The University of Alabama was a powerhouse football program in the '60s and '70s much like they are now during the Nick Saban era. "Virginia and Virginia Tech were not nationally recognized football programs at the time," Dwight said. "I thought it was pretty cool going to Alabama and being on TV and playing for national championships. Just thinking about playing for Coach Bryant I thought would be a great experience for me. Alabama was always on top for me. Sometimes I thought they didn't want me, and maybe they just wanted my teammates. I wanted to go there. Clemson came in pretty strong in the end. They told me I was their No. 1 recruit. I said 'okay,' but I never committed to them. I committed to Alabama. I still felt intimidated and really didn't know if I could play there, but I was going to give it my best. The whole ride has been fun, but I am still on the journey."

The 1971 season was Coach Bryant's 14th year as head coach at his alma mater. It was also the first season that African Americans contributed to the Crimson Tide varsity football team. Jackson was the first to accept a scholarship offer from Alabama in 1970 while Mitchell was the first to receive playing time in the wishbone offense, which was also the start of something new in Tuscaloosa. Five years later Stephenson arrived in a recruiting class which featured 10 African Americans. "I was very fortunate to be a part of a great recruiting class," Stephenson said. "There were 10 black players in our class. I think it was the first time that many black players had been in a recruiting class at Alabama. We had guys like Don McNeal, Curtis McGriff, Tim Travis, Wayne Hamilton, and John Knox. We were all getting in the flow of things. We were all having to get used to it. Everyone there had to depend on each other. We were a family. It wasn't meant to be easy. It turned out all were good people and good football players."

Alabama did not recruit the future Hall of Famer for a specific position. He was going to do what was asked of him. "They brought me in as a raw football player," Stephenson said. "It turned out to be the best doggone situation. Sylvester Croom had just been released by the New Orleans Saints, so he came back to Alabama and is working with the centers. I was working with coach Jack Rutledge and Terry Jones, who was the starting center at Alabama. I really had some great people there who taught me how to play the center position. We were upstairs in a meeting room one day. Coach Croom had three of us in there. He asked who can play center. I said, 'I can.' I went down and snapped the ball. Coach Croom said, 'I don't know if you can block, but you damn sure can snap the ball.' I still remember him saying that to me to this day."

Jones was the starting center for Alabama prior to Stephenson's arrival. It was his unselfishness and his love for Alabama that impressed Stephenson. Team came first. After retiring from the NFL, Jones has worked on the Crimson Tide coaching staff for more than 30 years as a strength and conditioning coach. His son, Terry Jones Jr., also played football for the Crimson Tide at tight end. Jones Sr. ended up starring on the other side of the ball. "Terry Jones should have been an All-American," Stephenson said. "I really played with some of the most unselfish players. Terry was the starting center during his sophomore and junior year. I came in during his junior year. Coach Bryant wanted one of us to play offense and one to play defense the next year. He put me on defense first. I don't think he liked the way I played defense too much. Big T went over there and did a hell of a job. That's just how unselfish he is. He could have gone over there, not tried as hard, missed a tackle, but he went over there for the team. I thought he could have been a No. 1 pick at center. He went on to play for the Green Bay Packers as a defensive lineman. He took a chance, and Coach Bryant took a chance on me. I was the starting center at Alabama my sophomore year. It worked out for me. It worked out for Big T and it worked out for the team."

Back home Stephenson's friends needed a little more proof before they believed he was the starter for the University of Alabama. "I'll never forget we had just finished going through spring ball, and Coach Bryant told me I was the starting center," he said. "I came back home during the summer. Some of my friends were asking how things were going. I told them I was the starting center. I told my best friend Kenny and a few other guys. There wasn't a computer back then. Nobody believed me. They picked up a *Street & Smith's* magazine. It listed Terry Jones as the starting center. Sure enough, we opened with Nebraska on national TV, and they finally realized I was the starter. We lost one game in 1977. We won the SEC but finished No. 2 behind Notre Dame. We won the national championship in 1978 and 1979."

Coach Bryant had heavy praise for Stephenson and described him as one of the best players to have ever played for him. Stephenson learned a lot about what Coach Bryant had to say about him but kept his distance during his time at the Capstone. "I don't think I even have a photo with Coach Bryant," Stephenson said. "I probably walked the other way when I saw him coming my direction. I'm really glad I played for him. I'm still carrying a lot of the things he taught me back then today. Did I go talk to him? Maybe once or twice would I go sit down with him. He would casually ask how my family was doing. I'd try to avoid him. I was intimidated by him. I appreciate all the things he said about me. It really was a great experience playing for Coach Bryant."

Coach Bryant spent 25 seasons at Alabama and won six national championships (1961, 1964, 1965, 1973, 1978, and 1979). He accumulated 13 SEC championships and defeated Auburn on November 28, 1981 to win his 315th game as a head coach, which was the most by any coach at that time. Dye, the head coach at Auburn who had been a former Bryant assistant coach at Alabama, was also the first to extend a scholarship offer to Stephenson.

After his sterling career at Alabama, Stephenson was drafted by Coach Shula and the Dolphins in the second round of the 1980 NFL Draft. "My father had this attitude that I could do it better than anyone," he said. "When people talk about male figures in my life, I had the best there was. My dad was a great example. He was my male role model. I was fortunate to have Coach Bryant, Coach Shula, and my high school head coach as role models in my life as well. I can truly say I was blessed."

He was the offensive captain for the Dolphins, which gave up the fewest sacks in the NFL from 1982 to 1987. He played in 107 straight games and started 80 consecutive games until the 1987 players' strike ended the streak. But then Stephenson suffered a serious left knee injury, which ended his career on a play involving former Alabama teammate, Marty Lyons. The New York Jets defensive lineman hit Stephenson from the side while trailing a running play, and Stephenson fell to the ground, his left knee locked, and the force of the weight on the joint caused the damage. He underwent extensive surgery to repair a torn anterior cruciate and lateral collateral ligaments. "Marty's a good guy," Stephenson told the *South Florida SunSentinel*. "He was just trying to help his team win. He didn't really see me. He just reacted. He came to see me. He seemed pretty shook up. I like him a lot. I know his wife and kids."

Stephenson tried to return to the field during the 1988 season but was forced to retire at 30 years old. He went on to form D. Stephenson Construction with his wife, Dinah, in 1992. It's based out of Fort Lauderdale, Florida, and also has offices in Miami and Delray Beach. He and his wife started the Dwight Stephenson Foundation in 2007, which is a non-profit organization serving the south Florida community and beyond. The foundation generates funding for a variety of charities.

Stephenson is most remembered as one of the best in the college and professional ranks. "I never thought all of this would happen," Stephenson said. "I am the type of person who doesn't want to be doing something just to do it. I want to be the best at what I'm doing. I want to accomplish more. I think all human beings are like that. I never thought I would be in the Pro Football Hall of Fame or be one of the best 100 NFL football players of all time. I just didn't know. When I came to Alabama, I knew about guys like Johnny Davis, Joe Willie Namath, and John Hannah. I could have never dreamed of being mentioned among those names."

CHAPTER 6

Marty Lyons

Marty Lyons played 11 seasons in the NFL with the New York Jets and was a first-team All-American for the University of Alabama. He started playing baseball at a young age and also expected to play in college until head coach Paul W. "Bear" Bryant made a comment, which would change his life forever.

Lyons moved to St. Petersburg, Florida, at a very early age after his parents, Leo and Thelma, decided to move from Takoma Park in Maryland. His father had retired as a police officer in Washington, D.C. Marty was the fifth of seven children. His four brothers and two sisters were Jim, Richard, Jackie, Dan, Theresa, and Phil. He came from a very athletic family, and the priorities for the Lyons were religion, family, and education. "We all went to the same high school," Lyons said. "A lot of the records at my high school were [from] my brothers. Just growing up and watching them play, I always wanted to be that good. Of course, then your second thought is: if I'm better, then I can break their records. The competition was always within the family. My parents were always supportive. We didn't have much, but every time a new season rolled around, we always had what we needed. When baseball season came, we had a new bat and new glove. Of course, if your bat broke, you were putting nails in it with electrical tape wrapped around it because it was the only bat you were getting that season."

Lyons started playing baseball in the second grade and continued throughout his youth and into high school. Football wasn't an option during his middle school days. He could not make the weight limit. His brothers attended Bishop Barry, an all-boys Catholic school, while his sisters attended Notre Dame, the all-girls Catholic school. By the time Marty reached high school, the schools combined to form St. Petersburg Catholic High School. Lyons did not expect the first days on the football field would take him so far in life. "I really didn't start playing organized football until ninth grade," he said. "I didn't really like it. I didn't love it. I didn't really want to do it. Being one of the larger freshmen, they moved me up to the varsity team when they needed bodies. I was more of a tackling dummy. We were doing the old Oklahoma drill and we had this coach out there, who told me to run the ball. I got tackled, and he told me to do it again. I did it six times, and he'd grab me by the facemask after each time and tell me to run again. He yelled at me at the end and said, 'Nobody can tackle you.' I told my older brother, Dan, after practice I quit. He said, 'You can't quit…if you quit now, you'll continue to quit the rest of your life.' He was right."

Lyons stuck with it and became a star fullback and inside line-backer for St. Petersburg Catholic. His career got off to rough start as he fumbled on the first play of his career as a sophomore against Tarpon Springs. "I was very fortunate to have a new head coach during my junior and senior year, coach George O'Brien. I think he saw more in me than I saw in myself. He would send out letters to different colleges, just saying this kid can play. There would then be a scout in the stands from Florida State one week and then one from Miami the next. All of a sudden, you are getting profile sheets to fill out and by the time you're a senior you are going on recruiting trips every Saturday morning. There wasn't a limitation back then on how many trips you could take."

The interest was high for his future college destination and it was led mostly by Alabama, Florida, Florida State, Kentucky, Maryland, Miami, and Tennessee. His first trip to Tuscaloosa certainly was not the best trip during his senior year, but it made a lasting impact. "It wasn't the worst but definitely not the most exciting visit," Lyons said. "Alabama was playing Virginia Tech at home that weekend. I think they dressed 80 players, and 50 of them played in the first half. Rich Wingo and John Mitchell were supposed to pick me up to take me out after the game. They never showed up. I went to bed and got up the next morning to meet with Coach Bryant. Coach Bryant said, 'I can't make you any promises, but if you are good enough, we'll give you an opportunity.'

"Other schools are telling me I can play right away if I come to their school. I'm thinking, *My high school won't even play all 26 of us. How bad is this program if I can play right away?* Coach Bryant was honest and truthful with me. The University of Alabama was also just far enough away from home. I knew if times got tough, I couldn't just get in the car and go be around high school buddies, be the big fish in a small pond again. Instead you are at Alabama where you are a small fish in a big ocean of fish."

When he was ready to make a decision, it came down to three schools. The finalists were Alabama with Bryant, Tennessee with head coach Bill Battle, and Florida with head coach Doug Dickey, and Bryant visited the Lyons home after Marty's basketball game. "I always thought if you are good enough to play, then go where the talent is the best and go where you are going to be challenged," Lyons said. "After the game I go home and I walked in to Coach Bryant having a beer with my dad. I think it was more exciting for my family and coaches at my high school to have Coach Bryant there. You really didn't learn to appreciate or even learn about his legacy until after you left Alabama. You don't realize what you are a part of. I know it was a special moment for everyone. Coach Bryant, personally, only signed two players in my class. I was one of them."

Lyons was always appreciative of his high school coach who helped jump-start his recruitment, gave him sound advice, and never encouraged him to go to another SEC school. "I was really most comfortable with Coach O'Brien throughout my whole recruitment," he said. "He was a big Florida Gator fan. I would go on my visits and then return home to talk to him about the trips. We'd talk about each school. He told me at the end of the process I can tell him where I was thinking about going and he would tell me if he thinks it's the right fit. He never pushed me in any direction. When I told him I had decided on the University of Alabama to play for Coach Bryant, he said, 'That's where you need to go.'"

It was a little eye-opening when Lyons' mother dropped him off in Tuscaloosa, but he had plenty of support and help. Lyons also knew he was not at Alabama just for himself. He was representing his family and all of his support system in St. Petersburg who had been with him every step of the way. "Everyone was proud," he said. "Coaches, teammates, everyone who put in the hard work. It wasn't just a scholarship for me. It was a scholarship for everyone. It wasn't really tough for me to leave. I got a little homesick, but it wasn't bad. I remember my mom and brothers dropping me off in front of the coliseum. I watched the lights turn the corner, and you realize you are starting the next chapter of your life. You walk into the equipment manager, Willie Meadows. You tell him your name. He gives you a basket. He says, 'If you want your laundry clean, you put it in here, or it's gonna be dirty. If you lose your jock, I'm not going to replace it.' Willie wasn't all warm and fuzzy. You really got to understand who he was the longer you were there.

"When I first arrived, I thought all the guys there were pretty special. They were only going to be as good as I let them. That's the mind-set I had going in. Not to say I didn't get my ass worn out a few times. You always tried to get better at each practice. I had one of the best defensive line coaches in the nation in coach Ken Donahue. He believed in fundamentals. He really helped me. I also have to give credit to my teammate, Bob Baumhower. We became very good friends. I lived with him. Just being his backup and watching him play, I really gained a lot of understanding about how to play Alabama football."

Freshmen were on the junior varsity team at Alabama in 1975. Lyons was fortunate to get called up to the varsity for three games during his first year with the Crimson Tide. He was also one of only six freshmen asked to travel with the team to the Sugar Bowl, which Alabama won 13–6 against Penn State. Lyons was riding high after his first year at the Capstone and knew his sophomore year would only get better. A lot of attention was on him, but it wasn't until after the 1976 season that Lyons fully grasped what it meant to become a full-time player for Coach Bryant. "When I signed with Alabama, I told Coach Bryant that I really loved baseball," he said. "He told me by my sophomore year I could play baseball. I dressed out every game as a sophomore. When it came time for Coach Bryant to award the A

Club letters, my name wasn't on the list. I was upset, to say the least. I didn't understand why I wasn't on the list. I dressed out every game and played in 10 of them and didn't get a letter. I walked into Coach Bryant's office to ask him why he didn't give me a letter. Coach Bryant is sitting behind his desk. He is smoking a Chesterfield, non-filter [cigarette]. I said, 'Coach, can I ask you a question?' He said, 'Yeah' and gestured to the couch. When you sat down in Coach Bryant's couch, you sunk about 12 inches. So, I'm looking up at Coach Bryant. I said, 'I just wanted to know why I didn't get a letter this year.' He simply looked at me and said, 'I don't think that letter means anything to you.'

"As you prepare to go into Coach Bryant's office, you go through your mind what your response will be if he says certain things. You figure there is going to be a little debate. Well, with Coach Bryant, there is no debate. Nine out of 10 times, he is right and the other time he is probably still right. I had my ace in the hole. I looked up at him and said, 'Coach, you told me a few years ago I could play baseball this year and I don't have to go to spring practice. Can I do that?' He said, 'Yeah, you can do that.' So now I'm feeling pretty good. I stood up, shook his hand, and started walking to the door. Coach Bryant said as I'm walking out, 'Marty, can I give you a little advice? Before you try to be good at two sports, try to be good in one and make sure it's the one you are on scholarship for.' And that was the end of my baseball career."

Alabama suffered an early-season loss to USC in 1978. Led by Joe Paterno, Penn State was undefeated and played Alabama on January 1, 1979 in the Sugar Bowl in New Orleans. Alabama won the game 14–7, and Crimson Tide fans will always remember it for the goal-line stand. Penn State quarterback Chuck Fusina asked Lyons how far the ball was from the goal line after being stopped on third down. "About a foot. You better pass," Lyons said. Fusina should have known the Tide's defense, which held opponents to fewer than nine points per game, was not going to let the Nittany Lions score on fourth down. Alabama linebacker Barry Krauss and Murray Legg drove Penn State running back Mike Guman back as he tried to leap over the line. Coach Bryant captured his fifth national championship for the University of Alabama.

Lyons finished his senior season with 119 tackles and 15 tackles for loss and earned consensus All-American and All-SEC honors. In addition, he was a team captain and the 1978 SEC Defensive Player of the Year for the Crimson Tide. He was also selected to the Tide's Team of the Century and part of the All-Decade team of the 1970s. He finished his career in Tuscaloosa with a 42–6 record and a member of three Sugar Bowl teams.

Lyons was drafted No. 14 overall by the New York Jets in 1979. He played all 12 seasons with the Jets and was part of a defensive line with Mark Gastineau, Joe Klecko, and Abdul Salaam known as the "New York Sack Exchange." The quartet led the NFL in sacks in 1981 with 61. Lyons was named a Pro Bowl alternate in 1982 and 1983. He registered 29 sacks during his NFL career.

The most meaningful part of Lyons' career has been his charity work. He started the Marty Lyons Foundation in 1982 after a week of monumental changes in his life, in which his first son, Rocky, was born. Four days later his father died, and his little brother, Keith, in the Big Brothers program passed away from leukemia. The Marty Lyons Foundation helps provide wishes to terminally ill children and has granted more than 8,000 wishes as of 2020.

Lyons was named the Walter Payton Man of the Year in 1984, which is presented annually by the NFL for a player's volunteer and charity work—as well as excellence on the field. He was award by the Heisman Trust in 2011 as the recipient of the Heisman Humanitarian Award. He may not have realized it during his time in Tuscaloosa, but Coach Bryant was preparing him for something greater than football: a feat he accomplished with his work with children in his foundation. "You didn't appreciate the values, his priorities, or what all he meant to his players until later on," Lyons said. "The further you go away from the university, the more you run into life lessons that Coach Bryant was preparing us for and all of a sudden you think, *Wow, this is what Coach Bryant meant.* He was preparing every one of his players for when the game of football was over for them to be successful. He knew some of us were good enough to play in the NFL. College football was going to be it for most of the guys. He gave an A Club letter to some a little earlier because they needed it more at the time. It helped motivate guys. Coach Bryant was a master at reading individuals and pushing the right buttons to get the most of each player."

Lyons was inducted in the state of Alabama Sports Hall of Fame (2000), Long Island's Suffolk Sports Hall of Fame (2001), Nassau County Sports Hall of Fame (2002), Maryland Sports Hall of Fame (2004), Tampa Bay Sports Hall of Fame (2007), and the College Football Hall of Fame (2011). He is also a member of the New York Jets Ring of Honor.

Lyons, along with his wife, Christine, have three children: Jesse, Megan, and Lucas. Rocky Lyons, his only child from his first marriage, is a physician in Wetumpka, Alabama. Marty fulfilled a promise in 2016 he made to Coach Bryant after departing for the NFL in 1979. He returned to the University of Alabama and graduated. Lyons has been a radio commentator for the New York Jets on

98.7 FM ESPN since 2002. "I remember thanking Coach Bryant for the opportunity to get an education and to play the game of football," Lyons told newyorkjets.com. "I was just drafted by the Jets, and he said in a very soft way, 'You'll be able to build financial security for you and your family and you'll play a game you love. But remember this: a winner in the game of life is the person that gives of himself so other people can grow.' I was 21 or 22 at the time and I didn't understand those words. They went in one ear and out the other. And in 1982, when I went through those six days, all of a sudden, those words popped back into my head about what Coach Bryant was actually saying. One day the game's going to end for everybody, but it doesn't mean life ends."

CHAPTER 7

Cornelius Bennett

Cornelius Bennett is one of the greatest linebackers to ever wear the Crimson Tide jersey. He was one of only two Alabama players ever named to three All-American teams (1984–1986), joining Woodrow Lowe. Although many will remember Bennett for his sack of Notre Dame quarterback Steve Beuerlein, Bennett will never forget the promise he made to his mother. "Playing at Alabama meant the world to me," Bennett said. "As a kid the dream was to make it to the NFL. I grew up watching my brothers play ball. We would watch football on TV on Saturdays and Sundays. I would always read about guys taking care of their parents. That was my dream. The college part was there, but the dream was to make it to the NFL. I remember my mom and I were watching TV one time. A commercial with a big diamond ring was on. I told her one day I was going to buy her one of those diamond rings when I made it. I feel like if I didn't have those dreams, none of it would have come true. I wouldn't have made it to where I am today if I didn't dream it. Every kid I knew back then had the same dream: to make it to the NFL.

"It was really more of a means to provide for your family, not just the football aspect of it. I loved football, but what kept me going more than anything was being able to provide for my family. That's the culture I grew up in: just helping one another. I played everything my parents allowed me to play. We didn't live in the projects, but we lived in a home next to the projects. I lived one block from the housing projects. Playing sports was my escape. I never wanted to be around all the bad stuff that was going on. Whatever season it was, that was the sport I was attracted to. I played every sport I could play, just anything I could do to stay out of trouble."

Bennett was born on August 25, 1965 to Lino aka Lillie Bennett in Birmingham. Bennett was bigger than most kids, and that started from birth when he weighed 11 pounds, nine ounces. "I have never been a small man," he said. "I grew up in a big family. There were six of us: three boys and three girls. My mother took care of her kids while my father worked for U.S. Steel. What my parents may have lacked in education, they didn't lack in being providers. They had eight mouths to feed. My father sacrificed family time in order to provide for his family. He would work a lot of double shifts at U.S. Steel. We always had more than we needed. Anyone who grew up on our block—cousins, relatives—they would come to our house if they needed a cup of sugar or a few eggs. They would come get something until they got back on their feet. That was always instilled in me, not fulfilling the dream of playing professional football but being a provider."

There have been different stories on the origination of his nickname "Biscuit," but Biscuit himself set the record straight. "It was around the fourth grade," Bennett said. "We had just moved from one end of town to the other. It put us a little closer to the housing projects. I was sitting at a cafeteria table in the lunchroom. I was with a bunch of the guys, and we were all cracking jokes. Someone called me 'biscuithead,' and it stuck since that day. The head part fell away, but the rest of it stuck with me. My family nickname was actually 'Fat Daddy.' One of my sisters was 'Fat Mamma.' What I didn't want to be called because of my name was 'Neil,' 'Corn,' or 'Corny.' I think someone in my group saw that it wasn't cool to call me that and I took offense to it. Everyone had nicknames back then—whether it was 'Fat,' 'Slim,' or 'Pookie.' Everyone in the hood had a nickname. I didn't want to be that kid who didn't have a nickname. I was a new kid in the area."

Bennett's size remained a hurdle throughout his adolescent years. He was always too big to play against kids his own age. "Kids knew I had a bunch of big people in my family," he said. "I didn't want to get picked on. I really didn't grow up fighting. I never looked for fights, and nobody tried to really fight me. I think I had two fights growing up. I think my size, and just walking into a room, nobody wanted to say much to me. I think my size was enough."

It wasn't until he arrived at Ensley High School when he could finally go against other players regardless of size. Bennett went to Jackson-Olin High School but lived in the Ensley school district. He played in a few games for Jackson-Olin before it was discovered and was forced to transfer to Ensley midseason and miss the remainder of the year. "I never really played organized football until I got to high school," he said. "I was always too big, I guess. There was also the financial part of it as well. I would always play sandlot football with my brothers, family members, or just other people in the neighborhood. Once I finally got to high school, I played a little bit of everything. I was tight end, running back, linebacker, defensive end. I even kicked and punted. I guess midway through my junior year is when I started to blossom. I was playing halfback in the wishbone offense.

That's when schools started taking notice of me. At least, that's when I think they did. That's just when I can go back and relate to when they started showing interest, and I thought there was a possibility of playing college football. In high school most of the positions I played was out of necessity to get the ball in my hands whether it was running back or tight end. I'd play cornerback or linebacker on defense so I could help dissect the offense we were playing against.

"Growing up in Birmingham, we didn't get a lot of NFL games, but we could always watch the Dallas Cowboys. They were always on TV. I loved playing tight end. My brothers were Cowboys fans, so naturally I became a Cowboys fan. When I was playing sandlot football, I always wanted to be like Billy Joe DuPree. He was the tight end for the Cowboys in the '70s. I played tight end the majority of my high school career. Halfway through my junior season is when I switched to halfback. I thought I was a pretty good tight end. I could run routes and I could block. I always wanted the ball in my hands."

Former Alabama great Bobby Humphrey was a few years younger than Bennett, but he remembers playing against him in high school. "He was big, strong, fast," Humphrey said. "I never got hit by him because he played running back and tight end. I never got hit by him until I got to college. I remember I tried to hit him a few times, but it never worked out really well."

Steve Savarese was fortunate to coach Bennett his final two years of high school. Coach Savarese grew up in Leeds, Alabama, before moving to Kansas for college. He returned to Alabama and had a 6'3", 220-pound athlete, who looked like a starter in college. The high school coaching legend, who was inducted into the Alabama Sports Hall of Fame and has served as the executive director of the Alabama High School Athletic Association, was the winningest active head coach in the state at the time of his retirement. Savarese also spent 12 seasons coaching at Benjamin Russell High School, seven seasons at Daphne High School, and three seasons at McGill-Toolen High School. "Cornelius was an outstanding person first and foremost," Coach Savarese said. "He had a great support system at home that helped enable him to grow as a person and as a man. He is one of the kindest people I have ever been around. He just loved to play the game. He was a great young man. As a football coach, you always try to get your best athletes involved. He was very unselfish. He definitely helped make up for lack of coaching on my part. I think even if he would have stayed at running back, he could have been one of the greatest of all time. He would have been great wherever he played. He just had such a strong passion for the game. He loved his teammates. He loved to compete whether it was on the football field or basketball court. I saw him guard [former Alabama basketball great and Houston Rockets first-round draft pick] Buck Johnson one night and completely shut him down. He was also a great baseball player. He loved sports and was just such a pleasure to be around. He was recruited by many people. We all thought he was going to Auburn."

The legendary Alabama star, in fact, committed to the Tigers at one point during his recruitment. Bennett does not regret his decision to go to Alabama but felt bad upsetting Auburn head coach Pat Dye. "I had committed to Auburn," Bennett said before Dye passed away in June of 2020. "Auburn just seemed like the best place for me to go at the time because of everything that was going on at Alabama. Coach Bryant had retired and passed away. The confusion of a 17-year old kid and the pressure of recruiting really weighed on me. I have always admired Coach Dye. I guess his relationship with

Alabama—coaching with Coach Bryant and just his upbringing—always attracted me to him. I truly admired Coach Dye and still do to this day. He is one of the finest coaches to coach college football. We still see each other. If you see us together, we have a player/coach type of relationship. You would think I played for him. I have such admiration for him and I think he would tell you he feels the same about me. Coach Dye would always jokingly say he would have won a national championship if I would have come to Auburn."

Bennett was recruited by first-year Alabama head coach Ray Perkins and longtime assistant coach Ken Donahue. He liked the recruiting approach of Coach Donahue, who had been with Coach Bryant since 1964. He did not attribute Coach Donahue to the reasoning behind his decision but was happy to play for him once he arrived in Tuscaloosa. "People who knew Coach Donahue would always tell me I must have really loved Alabama," Bennett said. "He was a no-nonsense type guy. My understanding is that he ruined it for Bo [Jackson] going to Alabama. At least that's what I heard because he was just so honest. He was a no-nonsense, soldier, Army guy. Bo asked him about playing as a freshman, and back then very few freshmen played. I think that's what turned Bo off from Alabama.

"I was happy I got to play for him because he helped groom me. For me, it was more of a desire and true want to. It was also a family thing. Birmingham was closer to Tuscaloosa. We were within walking distance to Legion Field. I also grew up an Alabama fan. Reginald 'Reggie' King was also a very close family friend. He played basketball at the University of Alabama. My mom and his mom were very close friends until his mom's death. We grew up across the street from each other. He graduated with my oldest sister. I think that relationship also drew me even closer to Alabama. We just thought it was best for me to go to Alabama as opposed to Auburn.

"I don't specifically remember telling Coach Dye. I know it wasn't face-to-face. I think back then I told someone on a landline phone I had changed my mind. It was hard because I was a shy kid. I didn't talk a lot. I went back on my word. I prided myself on my word. That was the hardest part, but so be it. It's a recruiting process. It's a difficult business for a 17, 18-year-old kid committing to something that is so life-changing for them. It's a heavy burden to bear. I luckily had a brother, Curtis, who went to school and played college football. My parents barely had any education—let alone a college education. They had never stepped foot on a college campus but maybe a few times to go see my brother. I was fortunate to have Curtis helping me make that decision. I think in today's world people are more educated."

Former Auburn assistant coach Bobby Wallace remembers trying to help land Bennett during his time on the Plains. "Cornelius was just a great, great athlete," Coach Wallace said. "He would play running back one week, defensive back the next. He barely played linebacker. Steve would put him wherever he was needed week-to-week. He was very versatile."

Coach Perkins was an assistant coach for a season at Mississippi State when Wallace was in Starkville, Mississippi, as a player. "I remember sitting next to Ray Perkins one night in Birmingham," Wallace said. "He was in town recruiting Cornelius and Curt Jarvis. I had both of those guys leaning toward coming to Auburn. I thought we would get both. We had some success recruiting in the Birmingham area after getting Bo Jackson and Jeff Parks two years before. I know it was a tough decision for Cornelius. I ended up on the bad side of both [Bennett and Jarvis]…Both handled it with class."

The College Football Hall of Fame linebacker was not really sure what position college coaches envisioned for him at the next level. He assumed running back since he rushed for 1,099 yards and 16 touchdowns during his senior season. He also averaged 10.1 yards per carry. "Coaches have to be a little more politically correct nowadays as far as recruiting is concerned," Bennett said. "Back then they told you all sorts of things to try to get you to come to their school. They were all telling me they were recruiting me as a running back. That's how I gained my notoriety. Coach Perkins will always say his desire was to play me at running back, but I never picked up the ball at Alabama unless it was from a fumble recovery or interception. I laughed about it with Coach Dye from time to time. Bo was at Auburn. He was ahead of me. Can you imagine a backfield with both of us in it? I was almost 6'3", 225 pounds when I stepped foot on the college campus. There weren't running backs that size back then. Eric Dickerson was really the only one. Bo wasn't that big. I really never envisioned myself playing running back in college. Not that I couldn't have done it. Coach Savarese was my high school coach my last two years. He thinks I could have been the best running back. I just did what coaches asked me to do. I tried to do it the best I could. I never wanted to pigeonhole myself. I'm glad coaches didn't either."

Bennett arrived at Alabama in 1983. The first-team All-American won the Lombardi Award in 1987, which was given annually to the best lineman or linebacker between 1970 and 2016 by Rotary International. The award is now given to any player regardless of position. He was also named the SEC Player of the Year as a senior. Bennet registered 287 tackles, 21.5 sacks, and three fumble recoveries during his college career for the Crimson Tide. "When I got to Alabama, it was because of Coach Donahue's no-nonsense approach that gave me the right perspective of playing college football," Bennett said. "There were no superstars. He treated everyone the same. He set up a great foundation for me. It was great to have him as defensive coordinator when I got to the University of Alabama. The practices were hard. They were brutal. They would probably be outlawed now. You just can't practice that way anymore."

Alabama fans will always remember Bennett for "the Sack." His legendary hit is still played on the highlight reel at Bryant-Denny Stadium before Crimson Tide home games on Saturdays in the fall. Beuerlein suffered a concussion on the play. "I'd been hit hard before, but not when I didn't see it coming," Beuerlein told the *Chicago Tribune* after the game. "When I got up, I saw mouths moving, but I heard no voices."

Alabama defeated Beuerlein's Fighting Irish 28–10 on October 4 at Legion Field. Bennett's sack in the first quarter sparked Alabama to an impressive victory. It also helped get the monkey off Alabama's back by beating Notre Dame as Coach Bryant surprisingly failed to do in four attempts as the head coach of the Crimson Tide.

Bennett maintained a close relationship with his head coach after college. "I still keep in touch with Coach Perkins," he said. "I was his ride or die, and he was mine. We came in together and left together. He was the one who had the vision to put me at outside linebacker. He coached Lawrence Taylor and drafted him when he was with the New York Giants. He saw similarities in our game. The rest is history. After the first practice, we always had that bond. I always appreciated him for being honest with me. He was almost like a second father to me. I was very fortunate to have that type of relationship with Coach

Perkins at Alabama and then with coach Marv Levy and Dan Reeves [in the NFL]. Those are three men I have the upmost respect for."

Bennett was rewarded for his hard work and dedication to the game of football, and his mom, Lillie, was gifted the big diamond ring her son promised her at a young age after he was selected with the No. 2 overall pick in the 1987 NFL Draft by the Indianapolis Colts. He was the highest draft selection in more than 20 years for Alabama.

After failing to reach an agreement on his contract, Bennett was part of a three-team trade to the Buffalo Bills. He played with the Bills from 1987 to 1995. He was a five-time Pro Bowl selection; three-time, first-team All-Pro; and two-time AFC Defensive Player of the Year. Bennett played three seasons with the Atlanta Falcons (1996–1998). He played his final two seasons with the Colts, the team who originally drafted him. Bennett amassed 1,190 tackles, 71.5 sacks, seven interceptions, 31 forced fumbles, 27 fumble recoveries, and three defensive touchdowns during his 14-year NFL career. He also competed in five Super Bowls.

CHAPTER 8

Bobby Humphrey

Bobby Humphrey was outstanding on the offensive side of the ball as the Crimson Tide's all-time leading rusher in a career (3,420 yards) and for both a single season (1,471) and game (284). Those records have been broken, but Humphrey's legacy endures. Many Alabama fans will never forget his 73-yard touchdown run in the first quarter at Penn State in 1987. The Nittany Lions were the defending national champions and were knocked off its pedestal by Humphrey's 220-yard rushing performance at Beaver Stadium.

Humphrey grew up in the Elyton Village housing projects across the street from Legion Field in Birmingham. "I was a single mom for the most part in the projects," Humphrey's mother, Marlene said. "It was hard. I was very young. I got married at a real young age. I dropped out of school when I was 15. I did the best I could to provide for my four children. I had very little to no help from their dad. It was hard to get a job to help with everything that we needed. I had four children by the time I was 23 years old, no car, no house, no job, no GED."

Bobby heard the roars of the crowd at Legion Field at a young age. The Crimson Tide led by Coach Paul W. "Bear" Bryant played many games at the stadium in Birmingham. It gave many low-income families an opportunity to earn a little bit of extra money. They allowed cars to park in their yard, parked cars for fans, or sold soft drinks in the stadium. "I grew up selling Cokes at Alabama games at Legion Field in the mid-to-late '70s," Humphrey said. "Alabama played a lot of their big home games there. The Iron Bowl was played there, the Tennessee game. That was what I did: sold Cokes and parked cars. I sold Cokes in the upper deck for two or three years. I was around 14 to 15 years old."

Humphrey did not know many of the players who were on the field for the University of Alabama at the time. Names were not on the back of the jerseys, but Alabama had superstars on the field, including players like Major Ogilvie, Johnny Musso, Ozzie Newsome, Dwight Stephenson.

It was hard for Humphrey to get permission from his mother to play football. Marlene was busy trying to raise four children (Montee, Bobby, Priscilla, and Noel) on her own and did not want the additional worry of her second oldest potentially getting hurt on the football field. "I didn't play organized football until high school," he said. "I just loved the game. I just loved football. We played in the yard all the time. We had a community team that I joined. We would always have a turkey bowl or snow bowl. It was 1st Street vs. 2nd Street. I was the little boy playing against the big boys back then. I just always loved it. My mom didn't want me to play organized football. She thought I'd get hurt, but she knew how much I loved it. She finally let me play in the ninth grade. That's when I really started."

She finally gave in one day after he stayed out well beyond the time she expected him to come home. "Growing up, I really didn't want him out there playing football" she said. "I wasn't too against basketball. I just thought football was a rough sport. I tried to keep him away from football as much as I could. He started sneaking away and not telling me he was out there playing. He really wanted me to be proud of him. He came home a little later than usual one night. I had my switch [a long, thin, stick used for punishment back in the day] ready. I drew back my switch when he came in, and he pulled two trophies from behind his back. He had won an MVP award. I sat down with him. He told me he loves the game. I knew he would play with or without my permission. I think it worked out pretty well."

There were several powerhouse football programs in Birmingham, but Glenn High School wasn't one of them—even with Humphrey in the backfield. It never had a winning season in 23 years. The Hawks (formerly known as the Rebels) had a 42-game losing streak from 1962 to 1966. "We really didn't have a lot of players," Humphrey said. "The largest classification in the state was 4A. We were a very small 4A school. We probably only had 45 players on the team. We didn't have a freshmen or JV team because everyone had to play on the varsity. We were everyone's homecoming game. I think we won a total of seven games during my entire career. I mean, we played some real good football teams. Cornelius Bennett was at Ensley High School. They were coached by Steve Savarese. Parker was a powerhouse. Jackson-Olin was really good. Carver was good. We never won against any of those guys."

Glenn High School may not have produced wins, but Humphrey was heavily recruited and wanted by most schools throughout the Southeast. He started as a sophomore but really became the focal point of the offense during his junior and senior season. He gained more than 7,000 all-purpose yards during his illustrious high school career. "It was during my junior year when coaches started recruiting me," Humphrey said. "I was putting up some really big numbers. I rushed for 250 yards against Ensley when I was a sophomore. I remember rushing for 303 yards against Jones Valley during my senior year; 200 came pretty easy. I want to say Coach Jim Fuller or coach Bobby Wallace was the first coach to recruit me. I am pretty sure it was Coach Fuller. I kind of remember the play that really got the attention of coaches. We were getting beat by Walker County. We were on our own 30-yard line. I ran a screen pass 70 yards for a touchdown. It got called back for a block in the back. It was one of those plays that got flagged when the play was all the way down the field. So they brought it back. We ran the exact same play, and I took it 85 yards around the right end on a screen pass for a touchdown. Someone yelled, 'There goes that kid from Glenn again.'"

Coach Bryant retired after the 1982 season and passed away a month later. Ray Perkins accepted the mountainous job of replacing the game's all-time winningest head coach and six-time national champion. Perkins was a former team captain, All-American, and national champion wide receiver from 1964 to 1966 in Tuscaloosa. He spent one season as an assistant coach at Mississippi State in 1973 before moving to coach in the NFL. He worked as an assistant with the New England Patriots and San Diego Chargers before becoming the head coach of the New York Giants in 1979. His assistants during his time with the Giants included Bill Parcells and Bill Belichick.

The University of Alabama finished 8–4 in his first season, which included a win in the Sun Bowl against SMU but a loss in the Iron Bowl. The Crimson Tide then suffered its first losing season since 1957. A win against Auburn helped, but the Tide needed to make a splash on the recruiting trail. Fuller had played alongside Perkins and was hired as the offensive line coach in 1984. His recruiting territory included the Birmingham area. "The first time I saw Bobby face-to-face, he walked out of the gym at Glenn High School," Fuller said. "I said, 'Oh my God.' I had a real problem here. He was dressed head-to-toe in orange and blue. That was the first time we ever met. I turned the heat up on him the first day I talked to him. I knew I had to do something quick when I saw that orange and blue on him."

Wallace had also played in the SEC, though he played at Mississippi State (1973–1975). He was hired in Pat Dye's first year at Auburn (1981) to coach defensive backs. Wallace was the secondary coach until 1985 when he became the defensive coordinator at his alma mater. Wallace was in charge of recruiting the Birmingham area for the Tigers. He landed his first big fish in 1982 when Auburn signed future Heisman Trophy winner Bo Jackson. Wallace was hopeful he could land another future All-American in Humphrey. "I started recruiting Bobby during his junior year," Wallace said. "He was a tremendous athlete. He was a very good basketball player. He was just good in everything. Glenn High School had a very small talented group. I think Bobby's senior year was the last year of the existence of the school. Bobby was a one-man show out there. If he didn't get it done, nobody was getting it done. He didn't get a lot of help."

The relationships built with Coach Fuller and Coach Wallace, who went on to become the all-time winningest head coach at the University of North Alabama and won three straight Division-II national championships, made an ever-lasting impact on Humphrey. The two coaches have remained in close contact with him to this day. "Just getting to know his mom, Marlene, and the family, they were just such quality people," Wallace said. "He was a lot of fun to recruit. I developed a good relationship with Bobby and his family that you hope to have. Our issue is we already had Bo Jackson and Brent Fullwood playing running back. I tried to sell him on the fact we could utilize everyone. We could use him like a slotback such as Johnny Rodgers at Nebraska. I think Bobby was smart enough to know he could be a marquee back. I think that was the biggest drawback, but Bobby would never say he was too good for that. He was always polite and cordial. I think Jim Fuller had the same relationship as I did with the family. I thought he did a phenomenal job recruiting him. We recruited Bobby as hard as we could have. I think Alabama was his first choice, but if Bo Jackson would have been at Alabama, I think he would have gone to Auburn."

Coach Fuller, who became the athletic director for Jacksonville State University from 2003 to 2008, enjoyed recruiting Humphrey and remembers the process going down to the wire. "Bobby is a great, great man," Fuller said. "He was a great young man when I recruited him. It was hectic because of the player he was. Everyone wanted him: us, Auburn, Florida State. Any time you recruit a top in-state player, you know it's going to be a battle against Auburn. Bobby took it all until the last day. I talked to him the night before. He told me he was going to call me the next morning. I asked, 'You can't tell us now?' We really needed to sign some good players. I waited throughout the night, but he did call us the next morning, and it all worked out pretty well. He sure was fun to watch. He really showed out on the field. He could run, throw, catch. Nobody ever questioned his speed. He had great speed, quickness, and agility. He had all of that. He wasn't shy on contact. He loved contact."

Humphrey still praises Fuller and Wallace. "I just had such a strong connection with both of them," he said. "Bobby Wallace and I stayed friends. I would go up and stay with him when he was the head coach at Temple. I would be on the sidelines with him. Coach Fuller and I also stayed friends forever. When he was the AD at Jacksonville State, I would go visit him. I still talk to both of them regularly. Coach Fuller called me during Marlon's recruitment to encourage me. He knew what I was going through. He remembered my recruitment very well."

The process was unique for Humphrey's family. "It was very different," Bobby's mother said. "I met a lot of people. I talked to a lot of coaches. It was very interesting. I felt pretty good about it because everyone in the SEC wanted Bobby. It was all very exciting. I talked to every coach in the SEC. A lot of them visited our home. It was fun but tiresome. I tried to be as nice to everyone, but the decision was all Bobby's, and he was going to make the decision on where he wanted to go. It was a blessing to me that he didn't want to go far from home. What really stood out to me about the entire process was just the presence the coaches had. They all really, really wanted him. Someone was always calling. I talked to a lot of different people who all wanted Bobby. We already had interest in Alabama and Auburn because they were in state.

"Coach Perkins was very nice. He made sure we knew they didn't just want Bobby, but they really needed him. He was always teasing. One of the times he visited, Alabama was playing at Legion Field. I told him that Bobby wants to go where he can play. Coach Perkins said, 'Well, Miss Humphrey, if we had a jersey for him, he can play for us tomorrow. We need him ASAP!' I will say the decision got a little hectic. I fell in love with coach Pat Dye…Even when Bobby decided to go to Alabama, he remained friends with us. I was just so happy Bobby went to Alabama because he was only 45 minutes away, and I could go see him."

Humphrey admitted that he prioritized the in-state schools. "I was really recruited heavily by four schools: Ole Miss, Clemson, Alabama, and Auburn," he said. "That's where I took my visits. Texas A&M recruited me, but not many kids were going out there from here back then. LSU wasn't getting too many top kids. Clemson had just won a national championship with Danny Ford [an Alabama graduate]. They were riding pretty high. I had a good visit to Clemson, but when it really came down to it, I was either going to Alabama or Auburn. That was it.

"I would say I grew up an Alabama fan because I grew up in the shadows of Legion Field. I didn't have a history or connection to Alabama, but I grew up watching them from a young age. I grew up across the street from the stadium. It's hard not to cheer for the school playing in the stadium right in your backyard. I didn't really know who any of the players were, but I was around all the fans and the people who were there to support Alabama. I thought what really sold Alabama is I felt comfortable there. It was a little bit closer to home. I felt the opportunity there was a little more clear. Auburn had quite a few backs at the time. They had Bo, Brent Fullwood, Tommie Agee. They were kind of loaded. Alabama had a lot of backs, too, but they didn't really have a solid starter. What I didn't know at the time was all the other backs who were going to be in my class like Gene Jelks, Murry Hill, Wayne Shaw, and George Scruggs. You had five or six freshmen, who were running backs or fullbacks in our recruiting class. You really couldn't keep up with those guys back then. You had no way of knowing. There was no social media, no Rivals[.com]. I knew Gene Jelks because we played basketball against each other. He played at Emma Sansom in Gadsden. I met him up there. All of the guys were great when we first got there."

Fast forward to Humphrey's freshman year in Tuscaloosa. The roster was filled with talent, especially on the defensive side of the ball with players like Bennett and Jon Hand. Derrick Thomas was also on the team and had entered in the same recruiting class as Humphrey. Humphrey was second on the team in rushing during his inaugural season with the Crimson Tide, finishing with 502 yards on the ground and a 5.1 per rush average. He remembers playing against Bennett in high school. Bennett was a few years older, but "Biscuit" barely played linebacker. He played running back and tight end and then became a dominant defensive player at Alabama. "He definitely hit me a lot in practice before I became the starter," Humphrey said. "Coach Perkins decided to throw the freshmen to the wolves back then. He wanted to test us to see how mentally tough we were, I guess. There was Jon Hand, Larry Roberts, Curt Jarvis, Wayne Davis, Brent Sowell, Randy Rockwell. I didn't know I had to go up against a pro defense the first time I was out there."

Humphrey had a breakout sophomore season for the Crimson Tide, rushing for 1,471 yards and scoring 15 touchdowns. Bill Curry became the head coach at Alabama in 1987. Humphrey finished 10th in the Heisman Trophy voting after his junior season when he rushed for 1,255 yards and 11 touchdowns. He was also the SEC Offensive Player of the Year. He broke his left foot in practice the following spring. The expectations were high for Humphrey, entering his senior season, and he was considered a Heisman front-runner. He broke his foot again early in his senior season, which ended his college career. He finished his college career with 3,420 rushing yards and 33 touchdowns.

After suffering a stress fracture to his left foot during spring drills in 1988, Humphrey reinjured it in Week Two of the season. So he entered the NFL Supplemental Draft in 1989 and was one of five players selected. The Denver Broncos drafted Humphrey in the first round. He rushed for 1,151 yards and seven touchdowns, threw a touchdown pass, and caught a touchdown in helping the Broncos reach the Super Bowl, though Denver would lose 55–10 to the San Francisco 49ers. He was selected to the Pro Bowl in his second season after rushing for 1,202 yards and seven touchdowns. He was the first Broncos player to rush for 1,000 yards in back-to-back seasons.

Humphrey spent a few seasons with the Miami Dolphins and was out of football for two years before attempting a comeback with the Buffalo Bills. He did not make the team, and his playing days came to an end. He spent six seasons coaching the Birmingham Steeldogs, which was part of the AF2, a developmental league for the Arena Football League. Humphrey currently serves as the vice president of business development for Bryant Bank in Birmingham.

Humphrey played football, basketball, and ran track in high school. It was a good thing he was fast, or his wife, Barbara, may have never noticed him. "I met Barbara my sophomore year in a high school city track meet," Humphrey said. "She went to Jackson-Olin. All the kids from Jackson-Olin were very fast. She ran a race she didn't typically run. She beat all the girls running against her, beat them at their own race. We made friends at the meet, and then I started calling her. We started seeing each other in the 10th grade, and that's where it all began for us."

Bobby and Barbara Humphrey, who went to UAB on a track scholarship, have five children: Maudrecus, Breona, Marlon, Brittley, and Marion. Marlon started his recruiting journey at a young age. He was a starter at national powerhouse Hoover High School just outside of Birmingham during his sophomore year. College coaches flocked to see him play. His offer sheet was lengthy with the likes of Alabama, Auburn, Florida State, Georgia, Mississippi State, Oregon, and Tennessee all hoping he would become a part of their program. He was the No. 1 player in Alabama. Rivals.com listed him as a five-star player and the No. 2 cornerback prospect in the country. It was easy for most to assume Marlon would follow in his father's footsteps to Alabama. But Bobby wanted Marlon to make his own decision. Bobby thought at one point Marlon would go to Florida State to get away from the pressure of being "Hump's son."

Florida State was also a top track program, which was a big influence at the time on Marlon's decision. He ultimately chose the University of Alabama and played for Nick Saban. He wore No. 26 at Alabama just like his father. As a redshirt freshman, he helped Alabama win its 16th national championship. He was a first-team All-American as a redshirt sophomore and decided to enter the NFL draft.

Humphrey was drafted No. 16 overall by the Baltimore Ravens. In his third year in the NFL, he was named first-team All-Pro and made his first Pro Bowl in 2019. His father was selected to the Pro Bowl after his second season in 1990. Both were selected in the first round of the NFL draft. "I guess the biggest difference between my recruitment and Marlon's is the social media aspect of it and the recruiting websites," his father said. "Everyone knows the details now of everything that's going on. Heck, they knew it before I did sometimes. So many people know about you. I was a good ballplayer in high school, but people out in California didn't know who I was. Marlon was nationally known. The social media and TV aspect of it is just so big. The talent wasn't much different. Now everyone can virtually see you. The media attention was definitely a lot less. It wasn't a big deal coming in as a freshman. People didn't recognize who you were. The expectation wasn't such and such. They knew you signed with Alabama, but they wanted to see how you performed before they pinned a bow on you. You had to prove some stuff on the field. Now guys come in, and they are getting media time without playing a snap. I never even made a highlight tape. We didn't have that technology. We didn't even watch much game film. We had those old spinning reels. Coaches were on the road a lot back then evaluating players. When I got to Alabama, they were still watching on those old tape reels. They didn't have VHS tapes. You basically had to go and put eyes on the players. I can't imagine that goes on too much anymore because coaches are so focused on their game the next day. It's very hard to do."

One of the best results of the Humphrey family came from the strength of Bobby's mother, who endured many tough years in the housing projects. She did anything she could to provide for her four children. "I always had one thing that was powerful in my life. I had God in my life," Marlene said. "I went from not having a GED to having a PhD. I went back to school. I accomplished several things, but I was happy all of my children received college scholarships and graduated. This whole ride has been wild, exciting, and the relationships even I built with coaches were very strong. I have friends for life. I'm just so happy and proud of all my kids and grandkids. I love them all very much."

CHAPTER 9

Antonio Langham

It was December 5, 1992. The game was tied with 3:16 remaining in the fourth quarter in the first ever SEC Championship Game at Legion Field in Birmingham. An 11–0 Alabama team faced an 8–3 Florida squad. The Gators were hoping to spoil the Tide's chances of playing for a national championship. Expecting to orchestrate a game-winning drive, Florida quarterback Shane Matthews dropped back and fired a pass to the right side of the field—right into the hands of sophomore defensive back Antonio Langham, who avoided a few tackles and found himself mauled by Alabama team-mates and fans in the end zone. Alabama defeated Florida 28–21 before winning its 12th national championship in the Sugar Bowl in New Orleans.

Langham would have kept running after he found the end zone on that pick-six if it wasn't for Minnie Pearl Jones, a close friend of his grandmother's, who made fun of him on his first touchdown when he was 6 years old. Jones may not have followed his scores as closely as she did when he was a lot younger, but any time Langham returned home, she reminded him of his first time in the end zone.

Langham was born July 31, 1972, in Town Creek, Alabama. His mother was so young that he was raised by his grandmother, Myrtle Langham, until she passed away when he was 12 years old. She wasn't the only one who took care of Antonio. The small town in north Alabama was home to around 1,200 people in the '70s and '80s. In many cases they all felt like family to each other. His mother's sister, Vernell, and her husband, Clyde Goode, had four boys of their own: Chris, Kerry, Pierre, and Clyde. Alabama fans definitely recognize the names as the Goodes were legendary. All played football for the Tide. Pierre won Mr. Football in Alabama in 1985. His mother's half-brother, Robert Penchion, also played in the NFL. "The only thing we really kept up with back then was the Dallas Cowboys and Lakers," Antonio said. "College football really wasn't on our radar. It wasn't even a conversation piece. I didn't really know much about Alabama football until Kerry started getting recruited. We heard about Auburn because they were recruiting Chris but really didn't think much about Alabama until they recruited Kerry."

His grandmother was a very important figure in his life during his childhood. She worked hard to make sure he had everything he needed even if there wasn't much left for herself. She was always a strong support system throughout his early athletic days. "If you come to my house, you will see a shrine of my grandmother," he said. "She raised all of her grandkids. I have to give her a lot of credit. That lady would be at work at 7:00 AM. She'd get off work, grab a sandwich. She really wouldn't have any rest. I was always into something: football, basketball, baseball. I'd make the All-Star team in baseball. She was always there. I was always amazed at how she put it all together. One of the biggest things I learned from her was responsibility. She had to be at work so early. She would always tell me to be responsible for my sisters to get up, get dressed, and get to school. I learned to do a lot of things at an early age. My grandmother did a tremendous job not only raising me, but also her other grandkids. All the grandparents in the community did a great job."

Antonio spent most of the time with his mother's family, but he also spent summers with Annie Pearl McCoy, his grandmother on his dad's side, in Red Bank, which was only about five minutes from Town Creek, Alabama. Life took a little bit of a turn with Antonio after his other grandmother, who raised him, passed away. His mother was living in Huntsville, Alabama. He went to live with her but not for long. "It was definitely a different type of struggle," he said. "Sometimes kids are hard on their parents when they aren't there. My mom was young when she had me. She didn't get to really live her teenage years. She had an opportunity to move to Huntsville. You don't really understand it as a kid, but we had our grandmother. So, it was good. We had a big family in Town Creek. I ended up doing a year in Huntsville around the seventh or eighth grade. I lived with my mom.

"I got really sick one day. My mom took me to the hospital. The doctors told her they didn't really know what was going on. I had really bad stomach ulcers. Maybe it was just stress. She told him he probably wants to be back in Town Creek with all his friends, cousins, and relatives. I was sitting in a room. I heard the doctor say, 'I don't know your situation, but if you don't get him back to somewhere he is happy, then you are going to lose him.' She called my aunt [Vernell] and uncle [Clyde]. She explained the situation. My uncle said, 'We can make room in here for one more person.' A guy from Town Creek came and picked me up. He brought me back to Town Creek. My sisters, Yolanda, Shonneky, and Tarshslyn, wanted to stay with my mom. They stayed with her. I stayed in Town Creek with Momma and Papa Goode until I graduated from high school."

Langham loved playing any sport at a young age. He wanted to play so badly that he was literally drawn to tears. Finally, when he was only about 5 years old, he started playing football for the peewee team. "I was always into sports," he said. "In Little League you couldn't start until you were 6 years old. Every day I would see my cousins walking to practice. I'm just sitting on the porch wanting to play so bad. My mom would always tell me I wasn't old enough yet. My grandmother would always say how she would be happy when I am old enough to play because I was driving her crazy. I would just sit on the doorstep and cry like a baby. I would get so mad and upset. I'd throw rocks at the door. I just always thought it was my mom's fault. I didn't realize at the time I wasn't at the right age.

"She goes out to the practice field one day. She told the coach, 'I don't care if you ever put him in the game, but will y'all please give him a jersey and let him come out here? He is driving me up a wall.' I think his name was Coach Green. He just started laughing. He said, 'Just leave him out here, and we'll figure it out.' I'm sure it was illegal, but back in the day in Town Creek, they probably didn't care who was old enough. They would let me practice but never put me in the game. I didn't care. I was on the team. I had a uniform. I had a gold helmet with the purple H [Hazlewood] on it. The following year I was 6. I was old enough to play. They put me in the game at running back. At that age your whole mind-set is to not let anyone touch you. You try to get away from everyone. I got the ball and turned up field. I started making people miss. I ran through the end zone and kept running out the gate. I ran all the way up into the stands, took my helmet off, and sat down with my grandmother [Myrtle]. The coach down on the field is looking at me like, that kid thinks the game is over because I ran a touchdown. My grandmother's good friend, Minnie Pearl Jones, laughing at me and saying the game isn't over. *Get out of your grandmother's lap.* Every time I used to see her—even when I came home when I was in the pros—she would always bring it up. She would say, 'Hey boy, remember that time you ran up in the stands and sat in your grandmother's lap?'"

Town Creek was a small town, but it was home to one of the best football programs in the state. Hazlewood High School, which closed in 2010, recorded the most wins (113) of any team in the state between 1980 and 1989. It won the state championship in 1981 behind Antonio's cousin, Chris, who rushed for 1,158 yards and averaged eight tackles a game on defense. Hazlewood moved from Class 1A to Class 2A in 1982. It didn't matter because it had Kerry and Pierre Goode. Kerry rushed for more than 1,000 yards and 18 touchdowns. Hazlewood returned to the state championship in 1985 when Pierre, a senior running back, rushed for 1,894 yards on only 161 carries and scored 32 touchdowns during the season. He set a single-season record with 233 points in 1985. Mr. Football in the state had also set a state record at the time with 85 touchdowns in his career.

Langham watched in awe for years the performance of his cousins and knew his time would come. He just didn't expect it to come as soon as it did. "I was on the varsity but was playing JV," he said. "I was playing free safety in practice. They were throwing balls in the air, and I just kept knocking them down or intercepting them. Our head coach, Jackie Ferguson, and our defensive coordinator, Jack Steele, looked at me and said, 'I don't know how you feel about this, but we are going to start you on the varsity at free safety.' I was like 150 pounds soaking wet. I'm looking at some of the other guys who are on the team. There were some big guys. This is a big-time program. Then they were like, 'Well, if you don't feel like you are ready, you don't have to play.' I'm thinking to myself, *Yeah, I don't think I want to play varsity right now.*

"I'm at the Goode house that night. I told them how the coaches wanted me to play on the varsity team, but I just don't think I'm ready. They all looked at me and just started laughing. They asked, 'So, you don't think you are tough enough to play on the varsity?' Kerry, Pierre, Chris all just laughing...I ended up starting at free safety and wide receiver. Guys my age were getting ready to go play junior varsity games on Monday or Tuesday nights...I didn't realize it at the time, but my coach told the JV coach just to let me go, but I better not play. I was given a uniform and just stood on the sidelines. I'm thinking I'm not good enough to play for the JV team, but I'm on the varsity. We played a pretty good team one night. They put me back deep to return the kick. I took it to the house. The JV coach told me to come over to him for a minute. I go to him and he says, 'You are done for the night.' The head football coach for the varsity was there, and he told him he better not put me back in the game."

In what was supposed to be a rebuilding year with Langham starting as a true freshman, Hazlewood finished the season 9–2 with a loss to Fyffe High School in the second round of the playoffs. A summer of relaxation was never the same after Langham's cousin, Kerry, came home one weekend. Langham had just completed his freshman year at Hazlewood. He was waiting on fall practice to roll around for his 10th grade season. "It was as hot as it could be," Langham said. "I was sitting around the house doing nothing. Kerry comes home for the weekend from Bama. He gets up Saturday morning and goes to the football field to work out. I'm in recliner when he gets home and says, 'So, this is what your summer consists of?' I was just like, 'Yeah, we haven't started football yet.' I hear Momma Goode in background saying, 'This is all he does. He doesn't work out. He isn't running. He's not doing anything. I know one thing: he better get a scholarship because ain't nobody around here can afford to pay for him to go to school.'

"I'm thinking my grandmother put some money aside for me in case I don't get a scholarship, but the money she had wasn't going to be enough for all four years. Kerry was like, 'Come on and work out with me.' I was like, all right it's not a big deal. I can go work out. I go work out with him. I finish that workout and come home and take a shower and pass out. We started jogging home from the field all though downtown Town Creek. It was the longest jog ever. I started falling behind. He just said every time he turned around, he wanted to make sure I wasn't walking. I don't even know if I ate that night. I was so tired. I just passed out."

Then Kerry went back to Tuscaloosa on Sunday and told Antonio to pack some clothes, a helmet, and his cleats for a few days. "My few days turned into a week. I'm thinking, *Why do I need my cleats and helmet?* We are just going to hang out. He ends up getting me into the Alabama football camp. A.J. Christoff was the defensive backs coach, and Tommy Bowden was the wide receivers coach at Alabama during that time. I'm there working out at receiver for the most part. When you go to those camps, you got to pick one position in the morning and another position in the afternoon. I'll never forget I was working out with another guy at receiver. His name was Chris Dozier from Marengo County. We are the two best receivers out there. All of a sudden, Coach Bowden has us running double moves, post corners, out and ups, stutter gos. He has us running routes his guys at Bama are doing. He came to us and said, 'You two guys can do it. I'm giving y'all certain routes to run I won't give other people.' I'm sitting there, and he looks at us saying, 'I'm going to keep my eye on you two.' I left that camp going into my 10th grade year. I came back home and told everyone that. They were like, 'Well, if he said that and you are doing all that, you might have a shot.' I'm now telling myself I have a shot to go to college if I keep working. That football camp helped. It led to a lot of things."

Hazlewood lost in the semifinals of the state playoffs the following season, but Langham did not want to see the same result his junior or senior year. He played just about every position on the field. He was also the kicker and nailed a field goal in overtime in the state semifinals against Cordova before beating New Brockton 28–0 in the state championship game. Langham's only loss during his senior season was to Class 4A Colbert County. He intercepted four passes in a 75–0 win in the state championship game against Georgiana. He had 15 interceptions during his senior season.

Langham was not the only star on his team. Tarrant Lynch was a three-time All-State selection and graduated in 1990 with Langham. He rumbled for 165 yards and four touchdowns in the state championship game and was named *The Decatur Daily* and *Times Daily* Player of the Year in 1989. "We had some really good players on each of those teams," Langham said. "We had Tarrant Lynch, who was a monster at running back. Tony Harris was our quarterback during my ninth and 10th grade year. When I was a senior, our whole class was so good that Alabama A&M said if we sign two of you [me and Lynch], we'll sign the rest of your senior class. There was a time when I contemplated it. I can take my whole class with me to Huntsville for college. That sounded pretty good to me. Of course, everyone else is telling me you better not turn down a scholarship to Alabama or Auburn to do that."

Colleges were showing a lot of interest in Langham during his junior and senior years. But even though coaches said they would watch him after his camp performance prior to his sophomore year, Alabama did not show much love. For Langham it was a blessing when Bill Curry decided to leave Alabama, and the Tide hired Gene Stallings to become its next head coach. He was also hyped up by Alabama's first African American quarterback, Walter Lewis. "Bama really never showed interest in me, to be honest," Langham said. "Auburn was showing a lot of interest. Miami showed a lot of interest. Coach Kevin Steele recruited me heavily to Tennessee; he always tells me about it. I was getting letters from Notre Dame and a few other schools up north. Coach Larry Blakeney was recruiting me like crazy to go to Auburn. He was like, 'Come to Auburn and you can play wide receiver.' My recruiting was different than most people. I didn't really have any free weekends. I would have to take my visits during the week. I remember flying to Auburn from Muscle Shoals on a Tuesday and coming back on Friday for a basketball game that night.

"I remember Walter Lewis is the one who really helped with Alabama. He was married to a young lady from Town Creek. He was working at [the University of Alabama] at the time. He told them, 'I know y'all are looking at Tarrant Lynch, but I'm telling you they have a kid who plays wide receiver and free safety. You can't teach ball skills like this. You are born with these type of instincts. Y'all just may want to look at this kid.' Coach Bill Curry was there at the time. He didn't think I could play big-time football. I really didn't get on Alabama's radar until Coach Curry left. Coach Stallings came through and said, 'I don't know what the last ball coach wanted, but we would really like to have you at Alabama.' I was like, finally Alabama wants me."

The choices came down to Alabama and Auburn, but he strongly considered Miami and Tennessee. Auburn Defensive Coordinator Steele was the defensive backs coach for the Volunteers during Langham's recruitment. "He was about as fun to recruit as anyone because of his personality," Coach Steele said. "I don't know if I ever recruited anyone with a more engaging personality. He was the same person you saw every day. He always had a bounce about him. He loved to compete. It didn't matter what it was. He is one of the most competitive guys I've ever been around. It was really fun recruiting him. People always told me I didn't have a chance recruiting him and they were probably right, but it was a lot of fun. I hope to think we made it a little hard on him. We kept our relationship from when I recruited him to this day."

Langham had heavy interest in the Hurricanes and was perplexed at the time when he found out they were moving on without him. "A few days before my visit, they called and told me they had pulled me off their board because they were told my folks and the people raising me wanted me to stay in state," he said. "They wished me the best of luck. I called Papa Goode to see if he had talked to them. He said he never got in any of his sons' recruiting business and wasn't going to mess anything up with me. It was pretty much the end of things with Miami after that regardless."

Auburn had a chance if head coach Pat Dye would have spent a little more time with Langham during his official visit. But Dye may have seen the writing on the wall. "I guess my decision was really made after my official visit to Auburn," Langham said. "I went to

Coach Dye's office to meet with him. He kept me in there for 15 minutes. Tarrant Lynch went in after me. They kept him in there for an hour and 15 minutes. I was like, 'What is it that makes them want him more than me?' I'd run into Coach Dye later on in life and ask him what happened. Coach Dye would tell me, 'Antonio, I'm going to be very honest. You grew up in a household with four other boys, who all played at Alabama. I knew I didn't have a damn chance in the world with you when they came on board and offered you. I thought I had a stronger chance to get Lynch. Of course, it turned out Lynch committed to Alabama before you did."

Bill Oliver, Larry Kirksey, and Woody McCorvey led the charge on the Alabama coaching staff for Coach Stallings to recruit Langham. Coach Stallings knew enough and sent his troops to see the talented athlete from the powerhouse in-state program. "What a great player he was," Coach Stallings said. "He was highly recruited. He was definitely one of the top two or three players I ever recruited. He was just an outstanding human being. I know a lot of people wanted him. He was an outstanding player for us. He made big plays in all the big games. He will always be one of my all-time favorite players."

When it came to his recruitment, there was a lot of miscommunication. "I really did like Auburn," Langham said. "They wanted me to play receiver. Bama said I could play receiver, too, and I had been going down to Tuscaloosa a lot because of the Goodes. I was just so used to Tuscaloosa. I was thinking maybe Alabama was the place for me. I knew people there. I was comfortable with the university. I was pretty much sold on them because I had been going down there so much. I think the night after Miami told me they were no longer going to recruit me, the *Times Daily* in Muscle Shoals was interviewing Tarrant. They ask him if he has decided who he is going to sign with. He said he was probably signing with Bama. They asked if it was a solid commitment, and he said yes. Then they ask if he knows what Antonio will do. He told them, 'I really don't know, but I'm pretty sure at the end of the day it will be Alabama.'

"Papa Goode always went out to get the paper every morning. You know what the story read? Langham and Lynch commit to Alabama. Papa Goode comes in there and says, 'Congrats son! It would have been nice if you would have told us you committed before we read about it in the paper.' I told him I haven't committed to anybody. He said, 'Look right here.' I said, 'Pops, I haven't talked to anyone.' He told me to go to school and he would call the paper to figure it all out. They told him what had happened, and that Tarrant said he was pretty sure I was going to Bama. Papa Goode said they should have talked to us before they did anything and made the decision for me.

"Of course, everyone is walking through school that morning telling me congratulations. Then I hear, 'Antonio Langham come to the gym!' I'm thinking, *What now?* Coach Blakeney from Auburn was in the gym. I don't know how he got to Town Creek so fast. He asked me if I fully committed to Alabama or if it was a misunderstanding. I told him I wasn't committed to anyone. I told him my commitment is still open. He said Auburn is still on the table for me if I want to go there. I just told him to give me some time. At the end of the day, I was just like, I'm going to stay with this commitment to Alabama. Honestly, it was a hell of a decision, hell of a decision. I can't complain about it at all."

Langham signed with Alabama in 1990. He was a member of the 1992 national championship team and a consensus first-team All-American after the 1993 season. He was awarded the Jim Thorpe

Award in 1993. Langham still holds the Crimson Tide career record for interceptions with 19. He was the No. 9 overall selection in the 1994 NFL Draft by the Cleveland Browns. He played for the Browns during the 1994 and 1995 seasons. He is one of only two players to have played for the Browns before they became the Baltimore Ravens and then returned to the Browns after the expansion team was formed in 1999. Langham's best season came in 1996 when he intercepted five passes for the Ravens.

Langham understands times were difficult for his mother when he was young. He has since mended things with her but can never repay his grandmothers, the Goode family, or any other of the people in his community of Town Creek for raising him to become the man he is today. "My relationship with my mom was very touch-and-go when I got to Bama," Langham said. "She never really came to my high school games. She came to homecoming during my senior year. That was really it. I didn't see her much during my freshman year at Alabama. I saw her a little more when I was a sophomore. The relationship was a little strained. I felt a certain way at that time. I don't have any ill will toward her. She was young. She was just trying to get back some of her life she had missed because she had kids at a very young age. You don't really understand that at the time. You are thinking your mom is supposed to be there. I looked at it the wrong way. As time went on, she was around more. Our relationship got to where it needed to be, where a mother and son relationship should be.

"Momma and Papa Goode are still there in Town Creek. Still to this day, people drive through and stop. They take pictures in front of their house like it's a museum. They point and say, 'That's the Goode's house.' Sometimes people will even get out of their cars and say, 'We are told this is where the Goodes and Antonio Langham grew up.' Mama Goode will bring people in the house sometimes. She will show them the trophies and all the plaques hanging up on the walls. People can't believe all the plaques."

The former two-time All-American for the Crimson Tide was inducted into the Alabama Sports Hall of Fame in 2009. He currently resides in Birmingham, where he works in radio and high school football.

CHAPTER 10

Jay Barker

It was December 2, 1989. The University of Alabama arrived at Auburn to play its first ever game at Jordan-Hare Stadium. Alabama was undefeated and ranked the No. 2 team in the country. A national championship, a potential first since Paul W. "Bear" Bryant had won his sixth in 1979 for the Tide, was in sight.

Alabama and Auburn began its rivalry in 1893 in Birmingham. The Tigers won that game 32–22. Games were played in Tuscaloosa, Montgomery, and Birmingham between 1893 and 1907 before a 41-year drought without playing each other for various reasons. The series resumed on December 4, 1948, and Alabama defeated the Tigers 55–0. The game was played in Birmingham and remained in the Iron City until the 54th match-up in Auburn between the in-state rivals.

Alabama had lost its previous two Iron Bowl games against the Tigers and head coach Pat Dye. Alabama needed a last second 52-yard field goal from Van Tiffin in the 1985 game to beat the Tigers. Bill Curry became the head coach of the Crimson Tide in 1987. Alabama finished 7–5 in 1987 and 9–4 in 1988 but with no wins against Auburn. The 1988 season is remembered more because of an off-the-field incident. Alabama lost to Ole Miss during home-coming in Tuscaloosa. Hours later a brick was thrown through Coach Curry's office window at the Alabama football complex. It seemed like the program had turned the corner as Alabama arrived on the Plains with a 10–0 record. Alabama led 10–7 at halftime, but the Tigers stormed back to take a 27–10 lead and eventually win the game 30–20. Alabama lost 33–25 to the Miami Hurricanes in the Sugar Bowl.

Curry submitted his resignation a few days later to become the head coach at another SEC school. The constant scrutiny and pressure on Curry opened the door for a converted free safety named Jay Barker to have an opportunity to play at the University of Alabama and for a future rematch with the Hurricanes in the Sugar Bowl in 1992. "I'll never forget the '89 Iron Bowl," Barker said. "It's the first time at Auburn. Alabama is up and looking to play for a national championship. Bill Curry leaves right after the game against Miami to become the head coach at Kentucky. It gave me a chance to play for Alabama. It gave me a shot and an opportunity. I promise you it wasn't me who threw a brick through Coach Curry's window, but someone did. It made him want to leave Alabama. He left Alabama for Kentucky. You'll never see a coach leave to become the head football coach at Kentucky instead of Alabama ever again."

Barker grew up just outside of Birmingham in the Grayson Valley/Chalkville area. He was born on July 20, 1972 to Jerome and Barbara Barker. He also has an older sister, Andrea. He started his football career at Center Point Park when he was 5 years old. His father finally gave in to his son, who constantly begged him to take him out to the park to play football. His father assumed Jay would want to go home once he was knocked down in the dirt. He didn't realize the road it would take his son for the rest of his life. "My dad was thinking, *he'll put pads on, get hit, and that will be it,*" Barker said. "I got clobbered the first time and I loved it. I jumped right back up. I started hitting guys. My dad said right then: based on my personality and the way I was reacting to the hits and running to the ball that I was hooked."

Barker would head to the Center Point ballpark for the next few years on Saturday mornings. He would weigh in, play in a game, and then watch older guys play throughout the morning. The University of Alabama wasn't playing on national TV every Saturday like they do today. Barker spent most Saturdays in the fall at the ballpark unless Alabama was on TV. There were times when he went with his family to Legion Field to cheer on the Tide.

Barker has been an Alabama fan since birth. His father was a big fan of Coach Bryant. It's rare for a son to go the opposite way, especially when you start out as a fan of one of the most storied programs in college football history. Barker will never forget the 1978 or 1979 national championship teams. He became a huge fan of Coach Bryant, had posters in his room, and had quotes on the wall of his bedroom. He was living in the state of Alabama and had the same dream thousands of kids have: to one day play football for the University of Alabama. "I wanted to play for Coach Bryant," he said. "I'd tell all my friends in the neighborhood I was going to play for Alabama one day. They would laugh. They couldn't believe I would say that. I'd tell them I wasn't bragging. That's what I was going to do. They all told me: no way was I ever going to do it. It pushed me and drove me. It made me work so hard to reach that goal. My goal was to play for Coach Bryant and win a national championship."

He vividly remembers previous games and former players who came before him at Alabama. He wore No. 42 throughout his Little

League and junior high days because of his childhood hero, Major Ogilvie, who starred for the Tide in 1978 and 1979. He was also a big fan of former Alabama stars like Steadman Shealy and Jeff Rutledge. He wasn't privy to just the offensive stars. He was enamored with Crimson Tide linebackers such as Cornelius Bennett and the late Derrick Thomas. He attended Alabama's game against Penn State in 1988 at Legion Field when Thomas had three sacks, nine quarterback hurries, and a safety. Barker was a fan at a young age, but he was an even bigger fan throughout the rest of his adolescent years.

The moment Barker learned of Coach's Bryant death on January 26, 1983 is a forever memory. "I was in fifth grade when Coach Bryant passed away," Barker said. "My teacher, Mrs. Prescott, was a huge Alabama fan. She and her husband would travel to home and away games in an RV every week. She would always come back on Monday morning to tell us all these stories about the trip and Coach Bryant. She walked out of the room and came back in. She was bawling, crying. We thought her husband may have died or someone in her family. She sat down. Our principal made an announcement over the intercom and said, 'We are sad to announce Coach Bryant has passed away.' Every kid in our school broke down and started crying. It didn't matter if you were an Alabama or Auburn fan. Everyone was crying because he was such an iconic figure in our state and so beloved by everyone. He was just such a legend. I'll never forget that moment."

Barker may have been one of the smallest players on the field during his middle school years and even his freshman year at Hewitt-Trussville High School. He was a 5'1", 130-pound football player during his middle school days and then only 5'4", 140 pounds as a freshman in high school. "I had been dominant all the way through my Little League years," he said. "I played at a high level. I played all over the field even during my ninth grade year. I was playing offense and defense. They put in me in at running back, wide receiver, free safety, cornerback, and outside linebacker. I had more of a defensive mentality. Even when I first started getting recruited, I was recruited mostly at free safety. The spring after my freshman year to the following fall, I grew to 5'10". I then grew a little bit more the next year. By the time I was a senior, I was a little over 6'1", 195 pounds. I grew even more when I got to college. I was a late bloomer. My son, Braxton, who is at Alabama right now is the same way. He was 5'11", 175 pounds in high school. Two years later at Alabama and he is 6'2", 210 pounds."

Barker was still rocking No. 42 during his junior season in high school, and it was by luck he had the opportunity to become a starter at quarterback by the time his senior season rolled around. "We had another quarterback in my age group who had good size," Barker said. "He was 6' tall in ninth grade. The quarterback position was going to be locked up by the time we came through. He all of a sudden stopped playing by his junior season. We knew we would be needing a new quarterback the next season because we had a senior who was leaving. Coach Wood came to me and said, 'I want to talk to you about making the transition to full-time quarterback.' At that time I was playing safety, a little bit of quarterback, returning punts, returning kicks, I was on the kickoff team and I punted some. I never came off the field."

Coach Jack Wood became the head coach at Hewitt-Trussville in 1983 and remained with the Huskies for the next 19 years and was inducted into the Alabama High School Athletics Association Hall of Fame in 2003. Wood ran a veer offense, which had two running backs in the backfield and is basically a triple-option scheme. Passing yards or even a pass for that matter was almost non-existent. It wasn't until a few games into Barker's senior season when Coach Wood decided it was time to let Barker air it out. "Jay, no doubt was a late bloomer," Coach Wood said. "He was always a great leader. He was very smart as far as studying and understanding the game. We probably should have gone to Jay as a junior, but we had a senior quarterback. We had some really good teams at Hewitt throughout the years. I think maybe his junior and senior year we didn't have the same supporting cast as some of our other great teams. He was a very good football player. He was very good on defense. He was very physical. I think he played at a higher level at safety than quarterback, but that probably had more to do with what we ran on offense."

Hewitt kept its offense the same throughout Barker's senior season. It would sometimes take out a tight end or running back for an extra receiver to go in the game. Barker didn't put up eye-popping numbers. His numbers wouldn't have registered on anyone's radar. He attended the Bowden Academy at Samford University during the summer prior to his senior season. Terry Bowden was the head coach at Samford. The Bowden Academy brought together all the Bowdens—Bobby, Tommy, Jeff, and Terry—for a football camp for quarterbacks, running backs, wide receivers, tight ends, linebackers, and defensive backs. It was essentially a camp for skill position players, and linemen were not included. Various coaches were asked to work the camp and evaluate players. Jimbo Fisher, who won a national championship at Florida State, was a graduate assistant at Samford during that time. Former Alabama color analyst and long-time NFL executive Phil Savage was in attendance at the camp while working at Alabama as a graduate assistant.

Barker had a big performance and set the long ball record with a 73-yard pass. Barker wasn't the only future national championship-winning quarterback at the camp that day. Former Florida State Heisman Trophy winner Chris Weinke also competed in the camp. Weinke chose to pursue a baseball career out of high school before returning to college in 1997 and leading the Seminoles to the 1999 National Championship.

Schools started taking notice of Barker. He received heavy interest from North Carolina State, Southern Miss, Army, and Navy. Florida State was also showing interest. Alabama and Auburn sent him the standard recruiting questionnaires, but the interest early in his senior season from the in-state schools was minimal. Barker started working with Fisher a little bit before his senior year on his throwing ability and mechanics. The longtime Alabama fan was finally noticed by an in-state school. It was Auburn and former Heisman Trophy winner Pat Sullivan who saw Barker before the Crimson Tide offered a scholarship. The Tigers had come off two straight Iron Bowl wins and would win its third straight a few months later.

Barker's game against Mountain Brook High School during his senior season became a pivotal moment in his recruitment. Hewitt-Trussville defeated Mountain Brook 21–17 in late September. "Pat Sullivan's son, Patrick, was playing quarterback at Mountain Brook," Barker said. "Pat came to watch him that night. He went up to Coach Wood after the game and said, 'Who's No. 11? I don't remember y'all sending me tape on him.' Coach Wood said, 'That's the Barker kid.' To which Coach Sullivan said, 'The free safety? When did he start playing quarterback?' Coach Wood said, 'This year. Our other guy quit, so we needed someone to take over.' Coach Sullivan said, 'Well, send me the tape from tonight because I want to dive in and send me whatever else you have.' That started the whole recruitment with Auburn. If Pat Sullivan wouldn't have been at the game, they wouldn't have had an any idea about me. I think it was a God thing. Coach Sullivan watched film from our game, he watched some other film on me, and they start recruiting me pretty heavily."

Alabama still had not picked up its interest in Barker. The Crimson Tide had its eyes set on other nationally known blue chip prospects like Weinke. Barker remembers getting invited to an Alabama game during his senior season. He traveled to Bryant-Denny Stadium with his father and met Coach Curry on the sidelines, shook hands, and that was basically it. There wasn't much conversation. Barker's dream of playing for Alabama was starting to fade.

He went through his senior season and started taking visits in January. Gene Stallings, who played for Coach Bryant at Texas A&M as one of the Junction Boys and was a former Alabama assistant coach, was hired to replace Curry as the head coach of the University of Alabama. Barker took visits to Auburn, North Carolina State, and Southern Miss. He expected his college choice to come down to one of those three programs.

Barker then received a phone call from new Alabama offensive coordinator Mal Moore. The former Alabama player, assistant coach, and later the athletic director who hired Nick Saban made sure Barker knew he should have been recruited by the in-state program long before the new staff arrived. "I remember Coach Stallings had his press conference accepting the job, and within about 10 to 15 minutes, our phone started ringing. It was Mal Moore," Barker said. "He said, 'Hey, this is Mal Moore. I'm the offensive coordinator at Alabama. I played for Alabama.' He starts telling me his background and how he played and coached for Coach Bryant. He told me how he has coached with Coach Stallings with the Arizona Cardinals. They are excited about being at Alabama. He said, 'We know you are a huge Alabama fan. We're so sorry they have not been recruiting you the way you should be. We feel like they should have been recruiting you from Day One. We went back and watched film. We want Alabama guys. We don't want guys from outside this area who don't understand what Alabama football is all about.'"

Alabama started recruiting Barker, Steve Christopher (who had just won a state championship at Anniston High School), and Jason Jack (who was also coming off a state championship win from Oxford High School). That's three in-state quarterbacks, two who had just won state championships and were invited to the Alabama/ Mississippi All-Star Game, and another (Barker), who may have passed for 500 yards during his senior season as a first-year starter at the position. Alabama was recruiting the in-state quarterbacks and targeting other in-state players who had not been receiving interest from the Tide like Antonio Langham (future All-American) and Sam Shade (future team captain).

Pat Dye coached with Coach Bryant at Alabama between 1965 and 1973 before becoming the head coach at East Carolina, Wyoming, and eventually Auburn. Coach Dye understood what it meant to play for Alabama, especially for a quarterback who grew up idolizing Coach Bryant. "I went down for my visit to Auburn and I'll never forget this," Barker said. "Coach Dye said, 'I know you are an Alabama fan. We'd love for you to come here if they don't offer you. We'd love for you to be a part of this program, but if Alabama does offer you, then you should take it. That's what you grew up loving and always wanted. I understand that. Alabama is a great place to play football. I coached there. I know.' He was very complimentary of Coach Stallings and his staff."

Curley Hallman, who grew up in Northport, hoped to one day play for Coach Bryant. He wasn't recruited by Alabama and went to Texas A&M. Hallman coached at Alabama between 1973 and 1976. He also returned for one season in 1997. "Hallman was the head coach at Southern Miss," Barker said. "He had a conversation with me that was very similar to Coach Dye. This was pretty early even before Alabama was in the picture. He said, 'If Alabama offers you, forget about everyone else. Go straight to Alabama. It's the best place to ever play football.' Those two guys, even though they were recruiting me, they encouraged me Alabama was the best place for me to go. They knew what it would mean for me and my future down the road."

Auburn originally offered Barker a grayshirt, meaning he would delay enrollment until the following spring semester of his freshman season. The Tigers learned of Alabama's sudden interest in Barker when the new coaching staff arrived and quickly changed to a regular scholarship offer. Auburn's original thought was to grayshirt Barker and then redshirt him because the Tigers had Stan White as the starting quarterback. White graduated from Berry High School (now Hoover High School) in a suburb of Birmingham. White started every game between his freshman and senior season (45 total) and led the Tigers to an 11–0 record in 1993. "I'll never forget Coach Sullivan talking to me about the future at Auburn and showing me their recruiting sheet," Barker said. "He showed me all the guys coming in and who they would have on the team a few years down the road in '93. He said he felt like they would have a phenomenal team. He told me to look at all the talent they were recruiting. He had a whole list of guys and a scoring system beside each one of them.

He said this team will have a real chance to win a national championship. He wasn't wrong. That team in '93 went undefeated, but they were on probation."

Barker took his visits and went through the emotional rollercoaster ride about where to go in the next step in life. The previous Alabama coaching staff had returned his high school tapes to his high school coach without ever reviewing them. "I went on my visit," Barker said. "I sat down with Coach Stallings, my mom, my dad, and I believe Mal was there. We had been there throughout the weekend. It was on Sunday morning. Coach Stallings looked at me and said, 'You are the first quarterback I am offering as the head coach at the University of Alabama. I'd love for you to be the first guy who says yes to the offer.'

"I couldn't say yes fast enough. I wanted to do cartwheels in his office. I had dreamed about this and worked so hard. There were so many obstacles in the way. I really thought I was going to play for Auburn, Southern Miss, N.C. State, or someplace else. The dream I had of playing at Alabama was not going to be fulfilled. So much had to happen for that to take place, and I thank God it did. My parents were ecstatic. They were so excited for me. They knew how hard I worked for it. My sister, Andrea, knew how hard I worked. The entire family had always been there for me, just so supportive in everything I did. They were at every practice, at every game. My dad coached me a lot in baseball and basketball. I just had great support system: spiritually, mentally, and emotionally, just knowing they always had your back no matter what. It was an accomplishment for me, but your family goes through all that stuff with you. It takes a family to make all of those things happen. It takes talent and hard work, but the support system is very important."

Barker was part of the 1990 recruiting class with the Crimson Tide. Because Alabama also signed the other two in-state quarterbacks—Christopher and Jack—there was uncertainty if Barker would play quarterback when he arrived at Alabama. Coach Bill Oliver wanted to bring Barker to the defensive side of the ball to form a safety tandem with Langham. Barker was redshirted as a freshman. Alabama welcomed an All-SEC performer in defensive back Chris Donnelly, who transferred in from Vanderbilt. He was a sigh of relief for Barker, who still doesn't know if it played a factor into him staying on offense.

Barker contributed throughout his redshirt freshman season as a backup and when starter Danny Woodson was injured. As the starting quarterback the next year, he led Alabama to an undefeated season in 1992 and defeated Miami 34–13 in the Sugar Bowl to help Alabama capture its 12th national championship. Playing for Coach Bryant did not happen, but winning a national championship with Coach Stallings was similar. "He was as close as you could get to Bear Bryant," Barker said, "as far as the way he talked, body movement, approach to the game, the way he was to his players. He was such a father figure to all of us. We had our dads. Some guys didn't. Some saw him as their father figure in their lives, a guy they could look to, go to, and talk to about certain things in life."

Barker finished his college career with a 35–2–1 record as the starting quarterback for the Tide. Alabama later had to forfeit its wins from the 1993 season after the NCAA ruled that Langham received improper benefits after signing with an agent after the 1992 season. Alabama finished the 1994 season undefeated before losing to Florida in the SEC Championship Game. Alabama then defeated Ohio State in the Citrus Bowl. "When they talk about win-loss records, I don't think there was anyone better than Jay Barker," Coach Stallings said. "He just did a super job. He was not highly recruited coming out of high school. I felt that was a mistake. I wanted him immediately when I got there. His strong suit was leadership. He would get in the huddle, call the play, and the players responded. It didn't matter if it was a run play or pass play. If Jay Barker was calling it, then it was going to work."

Barker gives a lot of credit to former Alabama offensive coordinator Homer Smith, who returned for Barker's senior year in Tuscaloosa. Barker had his best season in 1994 when he passed for 1,996 yards with 14 touchdowns and five interceptions. He also completed more than 60 percent of his passes. He won the Johnny Unitas Golden Arm award in 1994, was named first-team All-American, first-team All-SEC, first-team Academic All-American, first-team Academic All-SEC, and SEC Player of the Year. He was also named *The Birmingham News* SEC Offensive Player of the Year. He finished fifth in the voting for the Heisman Trophy and was inducted into the Alabama Sports Hall of Fame in 2015.

Barker also recalls a game against Anniston High School in the first round of the state playoffs led by Christopher and future Arkansas receiver Orlando Watters, who was perhaps the best player Barker played against throughout his high school career. There is one player who Barker will never forget during his playing days with the University of Alabama. "The best guy I played with at Alabama was David Palmer," he said. "There were other guys who had special things about them, but David was a special player not only as a receiver, but he was so dangerous as a returner. He could have played on both sides of the ball if he needed to. He had such an unbelievable ability to create plays and be there in big moments. He was an all-around utility guy. He could play receiver, quarterback, or running back. The air went out of the stadium when the ball was kicked to him on punts. Everyone was quiet. When he got the ball, everyone was yelling, 'Deuce! Deuce!'"

Barker's father passed away at age 51 to a sudden heart attack while Barker was attending the NFL Combine in Indianapolis. He died knowing his son was the all-time winningest quarterback in Alabama history.

Barker was drafted in the fifth round of the NFL draft in 1995 by the Green Bay Packers. He also spent time with the New England Patriots and Carolina Panthers. He spent 1998–2001 in the Canadian Football League with the Toronto Argonauts and the 2001 season with the Birmingham Thunderbolts in the XFL before officially retiring from football.

Barker is married to country music star Sara Evans. He has four children from his previous marriage: Andrew, Braxton, and twins Sarah Ashlee and Harrison. Evans has three children from her first marriage: Audrey, Olivia, and Avery. Braxton followed in his father's footsteps and joined the Alabama football team as a walk-on in 2018. Sarah Ashlee signed a basketball scholarship with the University of Georgia in 2020. Harrison is a preferred walk-on in football for UAB.

Coach Wood still raves about Barker. "I'm thrilled for all the success he's had," he said. "He was just a pleasure to always be around. He always had great work habits. He played three sports in high school. He was a hard-nosed basketball player and a good baseball player. You could see the dream coming. It was a lifelong dream for him to play at Alabama. It worked out well. He just continued to grow every year. I don't think some people realize how great he was as a senior in college. He was a heck of a player but an even better person. I wouldn't trade my time with him for anything."

CHAPTER 11

Chris Samuels

The University of Alabama had just lost a home game to Louisiana Tech on September 18, 1999. The Crimson Tide traveled to Gainesville to take on No. 3 Florida, and the Gators were riding a 30-game home winning streak. The overtime game went back and forth in The Swamp. The Gators scored first in overtime but missed the extra point. Alabama took possession on the 25-yard line. Alabama had its all-time leading rusher (until Derrick Henry came along) Shaun Alexander and the best left tackle in college football, Chris Samuels. The former Shaw High School Eagle bulldozed Florida safety Marquand Manuel to spring open Alexander for 25 yards down the left side for six points. The image is depicted in Daniel Moore's famous Alabama painting, "Rebirth in the Swamp." Chris Kemp missed the ensuing extra point, but Florida jumped offside. Kemp attempted another and made it to secure Alabama's win.

Alabama played Florida again in the SEC Championship Game and routed the Gators 34–7 and finished the regular season with a 10–2 record. Alabama was invited to play in the Orange Bowl in Miami against a Michigan team led by future six-time Super Bowl champion quarterback Tom Brady. The Wolverines won the game 35–34. It was the final game of Alexander's career in Tuscaloosa. Samuels didn't play in the game due to a lingering knee issue suffered during the middle of the season, which wasn't treated until after the SEC Championship Game. A little more than four months later, Samuels was drafted No. 3 overall in the 2000 NFL Draft by the Washington Redskins. Alexander was picked No. 19 overall by the Seattle Seahawks.

Alexander and Samuels are two of the best players to ever suit up for the Crimson Tide. There were more than a few twists and turns that led Samuels to becoming one of the best offensive linemen of all time in Tuscaloosa. His story includes a growth spurt prior to his junior season in high school, his teammate/best friend getting highly recruited, and a significant neck injury.

Chris' mother, Shirley, met her husband, James, during a trip to New York. James is a Vietnam veteran from Queens, New York, and decided to follow Shirley back to her hometown of Prichard, Alabama, where they were married and had four boys: James, Law, Dexter, and Chris. The youngest was definitely the biggest when he was born on July 28, 1977 at 10 pounds and two ounces.

When he was a 3-year-old kid, Chris started watching his brothers play football. He wanted to join them on the Pine Grove Colts peewee team. "I was underage at the time," he said. "My mom wanted me to go out and play just to do something. She asked, 'Can't he do something out there? Can't he be a cheerleader?' Of course, my older brothers were laughing and saying, 'Heck no, he isn't going to be a cheerleader.' Can you imagine me out there with pom-poms? I started playing the following year, but I was still underage. I was just on the team. I was finally on my own team when I was 5. I played quarterback, running back, safety, and cornerback. That was really the start of it. I continued to play until the fourth grade. I started having some problems in school because I was sick a lot and would miss some days. She took me out of all athletics until the eighth grade."

His mother was not happy taking him out of sports because she knew he loved it. He was a very good athlete at a young age and was always counted on by his teammates. The time he missed away from football, along with basketball, was tough. "Chris was just a real laid-back kid growing up," his mother said. "He was always a big kid. He never got into any trouble. Chris had really bad sinuses growing up. He would practice a lot during the week but never played when it came time for the game. Everyone was always saying, 'Come on, Chris, we need you, Chris.' He went back out for football in middle school and did really well."

Samuels has been close friends with former Alabama star Kelvin Sigler since the two met in the third grade. Sigler, who is now the defensive coordinator at Jacksonville State University, will always remember "Lollipop Chris" on the sidelines. "We never played park ball together," Sigler said. "I started playing in the seventh grade. Chris didn't come back out until the eighth grade. He played tight end and defensive end. When we went to ninth grade at Shaw High School, I was playing quarterback, and he was the backup quarterback. He started at tight end. We probably had the best recorded record ever for the freshman team at Shaw. We were 7–1.

"We were both on the varsity team during our sophomore year. I was actually starting, and Chris was our backup tight end. He was only 6'1", 200 pounds at the time. We used to have a team chaplain come pray for us before the game. He would always bring lollipops.

After we get done praying and start heading to the door, Chris would grab a handful of lollipops because he knew he wasn't going to play. You would see Chris with suckers in his sock, and he'd be sitting on the sideline sucking on a lollipop."

Samuels' athletic career turned a corner prior to the start of his junior season. He hit a growth spurt and became 6'4" and 240 pounds. After being discouraged as a freshman when he saw Sigler move to the varsity team from the ninth grade team, Samuels was now excited for the opportunity to contribute prior to his junior season. "I remember during my freshman year playing backup quarterback and starting at tight end," Samuels recalled. "They moved up four guys to the varsity team after the season, and I wasn't one of them. Sig was one of them. Then as a sophomore, we had a freshman, [future Auburn player] Leonardo Carson, take my starting position at tight end. I was kind of just on the scout team. After my sophomore year, the coaches pulled me into the office and asked how I felt about playing left tackle. I didn't care. I just wanted to play. I think the first game of my career at left tackle during my junior season, I was named the Optimist Club Offensive Lineman of the Week. I found my home at left tackle."

Sigler also remembers how quickly things changed when Samuels changed positions. "We had a great head coach in Terry Curtis, who left after our sophomore year to become the head coach at Murphy High School. Our defensive coordinator, Tommy Davis, was promoted to head coach," Sigler said. "Chris hit his growth spurt, and Coach decided to move him to left tackle. He became one of the quickest players out there on the field. He just dominated everything. He ended up having a really great high school career once he made the move."

College coaches were not originally traveling to Shaw High in Mobile to see the future NFL superstar in Samuels. They were going to see one of the best high school defensive backs in the country in Sigler, who had seven kick returns for touchdowns during his senior season. But then Samuels graded out at 90 percent or higher in each game as a senior. Sigler's recruitment opened the door—not only for himself, but also for his close friend. "Chris really didn't get noticed until later on," Sigler said. "Schools would come to see me and wonder who the big guy is at left tackle. He started getting recruited. We both ended up with an opportunity to go to Alabama, along with some other schools. We had been friends for a long time. We talked about going to the same school together. We also wanted to do whatever was best for each other. We knew we kind of wanted to stay together though. A lot of the same schools were recruiting us. Some schools thought they might have a better chance with Chris rather than me because of his neck injury. Some schools started to shy away when he suffered that injury."

The neck injury is something Chris, Kelvin, his mother, and many others will never forget. It could have been career-ending or even worse. It was a regular-season game against LeFlore High School. "I almost missed my opportunity," Chris said. "It was during my senior year. I hit a kid while playing on defense, and everything went numb and paralyzed. It was the final game of the season. I couldn't play in the first round of the playoff game against Anniston, who eventually won it all. I saw a bunch of specialists in Mobile. I learned I had spinal stenosis. Another doctor cleared me to play. A lot of schools were on me, but they backed off. Alabama is one of the few who never stopped recruiting me."

The stenosis, which is a narrowing of the spaces within the spine that can compress the nerves in the lower back and neck, was terrifying for everyone at the time, but later his teammates made light of the situation. "We were down and not playing well," Sigler said. "He got hurt, and it sparked us. We ended up winning the game. We laugh about it now when he hurt himself. Everyone was quiet. The paramedics were on the field. He was so big. They tried to pick him up and put him on the stretcher. He couldn't fit on it. He almost fell off of it completely. We always joke with him about it, but it was scary at the time. We were all down and hurt. He sparked us, and we made the playoffs. He was just a heck of a player."

Samuels will never forget when Alabama extended the scholarship offer. He may have let the recruiting process play out for a little while before making a decision, but in the back of his mind, he had always dreamed of playing for the Crimson Tide. "Alabama didn't offer me until my senior season," he said. "It was big time. I was a Bama fan. I remember the good old days. I remember back in 1992 when Alabama played Miami in the national championship game and crushed them. Everyone picked Miami to beat them. Alabama ran all over them. That was big time. I remember watching the game on a black-and-white TV with the coat hanger in there for the antenna. I was a big Bama fan. I remember Bear Bryant. My second oldest brother was a big Bear Bryant fan. He was an awesome coach. It was a dream come true when Alabama offered me."

Samuels and Sigler trimmed their list to three schools: Alabama, Auburn, and Mississippi State. LSU was a contender until Sigler decided he didn't want to go too far from home. "I was thinking I'm not going to go play in Louisiana," he said. "I come to find out later on that Baton Rouge was closer to Mobile than Tuscaloosa."

Samuels and Sigler enjoyed part of the recruiting process—games, unofficial visits, meetings with coaches—separately. The two, though, went together when it came down to taking official visits. The first stop was in Starkville. "I remember we had a really good time at Mississippi State," Sigler said. "Jackie Sherrill was the head coach. Chris was so excited because they were talking to him about tight end. Mississippi State had those big tight ends back then. Chris was all excited about that. I was like, 'Man whatever!'"

The next trip for the talented duo was to Alabama. Both had grown up Alabama fans but wanted to keep an open mind regarding their recruitment. Sigler knew his mind was made up prior to the official visit because of a prior in-home visit with Gene Stallings. The two discussed making their college decision together, but one jumped the gun. "My mom passed away from cancer during my senior season," Sigler said. "Coach DuBose was our area recruiting coach. Coach DuBose and Coach Stallings came to my house. Coach Stallings asked me where my mom was when he was there. She was bedridden at the time. She had chemo, lost all her hair, couldn't walk, couldn't talk. He went in there and held her hand for 20 to 30 minutes just talking to her. She didn't know him from the man on the moon. I made up in my head that's where I'm going.

"We then had a really good visit to Alabama that next weekend. I remember Deshea Townsend was my player host. Before we met with Coach Stallings, Chris said to me, 'Now we aren't going to commit. We are still going to take our visit to Auburn next weekend.' Coach Joe Whitt was recruiting us. We both really liked him. He was from Mobile. He played at Blount High School. My family had gone to school with Coach Whitt, so we are going to still take that visit. Coach Stallings starts talking to me. He said, 'We want you!' I just shouted, 'I'm coming, Coach!' Then I was like, 'Well, hold up. Don't tell anyone yet.' I told Coach Stallings, 'Chris really wanted to visit Auburn next week, and I promised I would go with him.' So I came out of his office. Chris asked how it went. I told him I committed. He said, 'I thought we were going to wait?' I was just like, 'Sorry, man.' He didn't end up committing that weekend with me."

Samuels was a little surprised after Sigler walked out of Coach Stallings' office, but of course, it wasn't going to change their friendship. "My journey with Sig was always great," he said. "That's my buddy. We started playing football together in eighth grade. We received scholarships together. We went on our visits together. He was a Bama fan his whole life. We said we were going to commit together. Then, he goes and commits during the visit to Bama. Coach Stallings is now trying to get me to commit. I was like I want to still take visits and party a little bit. Sig told me not to tell anyone. We are like brothers. We have been through a lot together."

Samuels' reason for wanting to visit Auburn was more out of respect for Whitt, who had been an Auburn assistant coach for 25 years, than anything else. Coach Whitt was also the first coach to ever call Samuels. It had made a significant impact on him, but in the end, the opportunity to play for the team he rooted for since childhood was too much to overcome.

"We went back to school that next Monday," Sigler said. "Coaches are always calling you to come to office to talk to coaches. It's a little different now than it was back then. We weren't really into recruiting. We hated traveling. We got tired of getting called out of class to talk to coaches. I think a coach from Southern Miss asked Chris one day who was recruiting him from Alabama. Chris said 'Mike DuBose.' The coach said, 'Well, you call Mike DuBose and tell him I will whoop his ass.' It was funny."

What was less amusing was having to have a serious conversation with Whitt. "We both got phone calls that Monday morning after the Alabama visit," Sigler said. "Chris said to our head coach, Coach Davis, he was tired of all this. He looked at me. I said, 'Well, you already know what I did.' Chris said, 'Coach, Sig committed to Alabama this weekend. I am tired of going on these visits and coaches calling me out of class.' He said, 'I am ready to commit to Alabama too.' Coach Davis said, 'Well, if that's what y'all want to do, you need to be a man and call Coach Whitt. Tell him you appreciate the opportunity and tell him what you are going to do.' So we called Coach Whitt. We told him, 'We appreciated everything he did, but we both said we are going to the University of Alabama.' We weren't going to take a trip to Auburn. He respected us for the call. He told us 'good luck,' and that was that."

Alabama could have moved on from Samuels. It stood by him during a tough time at the conclusion of his senior season when he wasn't sure if his playing days had ended. "It was special," he said. "I would have been successful regardless if I was coaching ball or if I went to a smaller college. I was blessed to play at Alabama. Alabama is known for having some of the best players in college football. I was playing against guys at the highest level. I was playing against guys who played for Auburn, Florida, LSU. Even with my neck injury, Alabama never quit on me. They gave me a chance. They believed in me. Thank God I never had serious injuries with my neck while I was there. I had a great career, great experience."

Samuels also will never forget that Alabama stood by his side even after his playing days ended in the NFL. The school honored his scholarship. "I was a poor student. I came back and got my degree after I finished my NFL career. They stuck with me even on that," Samuels said. "I didn't have to pay anything. This time around I was a grown man, very mature. I was married with a child. I went back and made straight As and I made the dean's list. It was something I could have done the first time, but I was young and immature. I am blessed they still honored the scholarship. Coach Saban gave me the chance to work under him while I went back to school."

When he was a true freshman at Alabama in 1995, Samuels reverted back to his early days of high school. He was redshirted. He was not sure when he would blossom into the player he was during his junior and senior year of high school. He questioned his skills and if he would even make it to the NFL one day. "When I first got to Alabama, I was out of shape," Samuels said. "I really took things for granted. I was a crybaby. Coach DuBose, Coach Calloway—those guys really rode me. I ended up having a good career, but I wasn't ready my first year. I was mentally weak. I was not in great shape. I really couldn't finish the drills. I wasn't mentally tough enough. I got redshirted. The next year going through spring, I got to a point where I was fed up being the guy in the corner doing bear crawls by myself because I couldn't keep up with the rest of the guys. I had a really good redshirt freshman year. I got a lot of playing time. I eventually started my redshirt freshman year and started every game since then.

"I used to go up against these guys like Shannon Brown and I could barely block them. I'm thinking in my head, *These are big-time guys.* Some of them got cut in the NFL, and I'm thinking, *How am I ever going to make it?* Darrell Blackburn was all-everything at Alabama at the time. I started improving in the weight room, and my mental toughness was better. I blocked him in the spring and did a pretty good job. He was a projected first rounder, but he ended up having some kidney issues and had to stop playing. I started thinking to myself, *If I can block him, then I have a chance.* I was hard as steel when I left Alabama. Coach Terry Jones did a great job with us. Once I got in the pros, no matter what adversity I went through, I knew how to respond because the guys at Alabama made me a man and prepared me for the next level.

"I'll never forget this one thing that happened my freshman year at Alabama, though. Coach Stallings was big time. He demanded respect as soon as he walked into the room. He was just an awesome coach. I remember my first year there we did all these sprints after practice. I was pushing toward the tail end on most of them. The last sprint I burst out of the pack and led the whole thing. I'm thinking I had just done something good. He said, 'Hey 60, doesn't mean anything if you run it on the last one. I want you to sprint them all from the beginning. Give everything you got at the start.' He was making a good point. I was holding back."

Samuels started 42 consecutive games at Alabama at left tackle. He won the Outland Trophy in 1999 given annually to the nation's top lineman. He was a first-team All-American, first-team All-SEC, and won the Jacobs Award, which is given annually to the SEC's most outstanding blocker. Samuels started 42 straight games without giving up a sack.

He was chosen team captain during his 10-year career in the NFL with the Redskins. He was a six-time Pro Bowl selection. He suffered temporary upper-body paralysis due to compression on his neck from a helmet-to-helmet hit while in pass protection against the Carolina Panthers on October 11, 2009. The injury was related to his spinal stenosis, and he retired from the NFL on March 4, 2010 based on advice from doctors due to risk of potential long-term injury. Samuels was inducted into the Redskins' Ring of Fame in 2019. He was also inducted into the Alabama Sports Hall of Fame in 2016.

When Samuels retired from professional football, he joined Sigler's staff as an assistant coach in Mobile before the two joined Alabama's coaching staff. Samuels currently resides in Potomac, Maryland, with his wife, Monique, and their three children, Christopher, Milani, and Chase. Samuels continues to work in high school football. His older brother, Law, played in the Arena Football League from 1994 through 2010 as a wide receiver and linebacker. He was inducted into the Arena Football League Hall of Fame in 2013.

Samuels and Sigler remain close friends to this day. "Sig and I went through a lot together," Samuels said. "We've been through the good and the bad. His mother passed away from cancer when we were seniors in high school. That was tough for him. We went to college together and had great times. I'm just so proud of him. He could have definitely made it to the pros like me if he didn't have a knee injury. He is now the defensive coordinator at Jacksonville State. I got to coach with him at Blount High School, and then we both worked together for Coach Saban. Coach Saban really helped both of us out a lot. I've had college and pro coaching opportunities because of Coach Saban. I'm happy Sig and I were able to do so many things together."

CHAPTER 12

Brodie Croyle

The roar of the crowd filled the gymnasium at Westbrook Christian School in Rainbow City, Alabama, when Brodie Croyle announced his commitment to the University of Alabama in December of 2000. Croyle knows it may have been a low-level golf clap if he had announced for Florida State. Croyle's father walked outside the gym, following the announcement, with his hands in the air to let out a loud yell of happiness.

It was a dark time for the football program at the University of Alabama. The high school record-setting quarterback was a glimmer of hope and a spark that might help extinguish the bad taste from the end of the DuBose era at Alabama. The gymnasium was filled with the entire K-12 student body, teachers, coaches, administrators, parents, and TV cameras from numerous news outlets.

This was my first experience of watching a live announcement. We were high school teammates. I was lucky enough to play a full season with Croyle as a freshman. Westbrook is a small private school and moved to Class 2A prior to Croyle's senior year. There was definitely a lot of buzz around the 2000 season as one of the top prep quarterbacks in the country looked to break more state records with an explosive offense.

The high expectations of the season abruptly came to end during the first quarter of the first game of Croyle's senior year. He scrambled after getting chased in the backfield, planted, and went down. The stadium was in complete silence. Croyle was tough and lived by the mantra to always get up and he did. The Class 3A Yellow Jackets defeated the Westbrook Warriors that night. Croyle later returned to the sidelines on crutches. The diagnosis of a torn ACL put him out for the year. The backup quarterback tore his ACL the following week, and Westbrook finished the season 3–7.

Croyle passed for 9,323 yards with 105 touchdowns (both state records at the time) and only played half a quarter as a senior. When he graduated he also held the state record for passing yards in a season (3,787), single game (528), touchdown passes in a season (44), and touchdown passes in a game (seven).

There was obvious concern about how this injury might impact that potential. The cult-classic football movie *Varsity Blues* had come out the previous year. Star quarterback Lance Harbor played by Paul Walker (RIP) tore up his knee, and all was lost, including his scholarship to Florida State. That's what most of us were thinking. Maybe Croyle's career had come to an end. But his sports career didn't come to an end. It was just beginning.

Croyle was an Alabama legacy. His father, John, was an All-American defensive end for Paul W. "Bear" Bryant and helped the Crimson Tide to the national championship in 1973. His sister, Reagan, played basketball for Alabama and was the homecoming queen in 1999. She is also married to former Alabama quarterback John David Phillips. From attending countless games, to hearing about his father playing for Coach Bryant, to always dreaming of playing for the Tide, Croyle knew about Alabama his entire life. Following in the same footsteps of Alabama legends such as Joe Namath, Kenny Stabler, Jay Barker, and Pat Trammell was expected once he became a national quarterback prospect. However, his path to Alabama wasn't as cut and dry as most outsiders would have predicted. In fact, Alabama was not his first choice.

The original connection between the Croyle family and Alabama started when his father, John, attended a basketball camp in Tuscaloosa prior to his sophomore year in high school in Gadsden. Coach Bryant took notice of the tall, lanky 6'4", 185-pound wide receiver. John met Coach Bryant, who told him that day, "We'll be watching." "I ended up having a pretty good junior season," John Croyle said. "I took some visits, and a few other schools were in the hunt, but they were always a distant second to Alabama. There was just this air about Coach Bryant. You wanted to play for him. I remember there were three guys [from Gadsden], who were down at Alabama at the time: Danny Ford, Steve Clay, and Wayne Stevens. They took me out during the Christmas holidays my senior year and convinced me Alabama is where I needed to go. I don't know if Coach Bryant had anything to do with that. I called [Alabama defensive ends coach] Dude Hennessey. I said, 'I'd like to come to Alabama.' He said, 'That's fine.' That was pretty much it. People will say stuff to me now about Coach Bryant and Alabama. It all goes back to, 'We'll be watching you.'"

During John's playing days for the Tide, he worked as a youth counselor at King's Arrow Ranch for Boys in Lumberton, Mississippi. He was a defensive star for Alabama and finished his senior season in 1973 as a national champion. He had an opportunity to further his career in the NFL but instead embarked on a different journey. "I came to Alabama as a little kid," he said. "My life changed, and my life's work was instrumental in the advice I received while I was there. I really wasn't sure what I wanted to do. I told Coach Bryant I had this idea of opening a boy's ranch. Coach Bryant put his hand up and said, 'Go build that boy's ranch.'"

He walked away from football and opened the Big Oak Ranch in 1974 just outside of Gadsden. John had met his wife Teresa (Tee) at 12th Street Baptist Church in Gadsden when the two were in the same nursery school class, and they have been together ever since. Best friends in high school, they married shortly after John opened the ranch. "I told her three things: 'I love you, will you marry me, and we will have 80 children!' She said yes to all three. She's had every reason to leave me, but she hasn't yet."

The Big Oak Ranch has been home to more than 2,000 children with the boy's ranch and the girl's ranch (established in 1988 in Springville, Alabama). It has also been home to John and Tee's biological children, Reagan and Brodie. "I went straight from the hospital to the ranch," Brodie said. "It's truly the only life I've ever known. Growing up there teaches you so much about life but also gives you perspective about life as well. I never knew it any differently. Those were my brothers and sisters. They were no different than me. The only difference is I had a mom and dad, and they didn't. I am very grateful to have grown up there. It was a blessing to me, which obviously shaped so many things in my life. I didn't realize it at the time, but it was teaching me so many things about life, leadership, and just understanding what makes people tick. There are a lot of personalities living on a ranch with 100 other kids. Back then, I was always John's son. If one of the guys [on the ranch] got in trouble with John, they took it out on Brodie. People always ask, 'Where do you get your toughness?' Well, I've been hit by people who are 17, 18 years old since I was 10-years old."

John knew about his son's toughness long before the older guys were taking out their frustrations in the fields at the Big Oak Ranch. It started when he was very young and when Brodie said he wanted to play in the NFL one day. John was 100 percent behind him, even though Brodie had never played organized football. "He was 2 years old, and we had a little slope in our yard," his father said. "He had training wheels on his bicycle. He kept begging me to take the training wheels off. I said, 'All right.' I rolled him down the hill, and he crashed. He got up and went down the slope again without the training wheels again. He made it. I looked at his momma and said, 'That's not normal.' There were things throughout his childhood he could do well—whether it was football or baseball. He played basketball more just for fun. He just had a natural gift to throw. He came to me around 11 years old and said, 'One day I'm going to play in the NFL.' I looked at him and said, 'Okay, bud, let's go for it.' I was thinking in my mind: *You've never played a down of football. You've never played a real football game.* But his mind was made up."

Brodie remembers telling his parents of his goals and aspirations. He was building his confidence, but it also consumed him. He wanted to become a star football player, a high school All-American, a college football standout, and then an NFL player. "I remember when I told my parents I wanted to play in the NFL after just playing tackle football in the yard," he said. "They told me to, 'Go for it, big dog.' Shoot for the moon. I am ashamed to say football became my God. It was tunnel vision. It's all I thought about. It's all I wanted. I played JV football. I wanted to play wide receiver, but they thought

I could throw it better than I could catch. I started at quarterback as an eighth grader on the varsity football team."

The pressure of starting an actual game prior to starting your first day in high school may have worried some athletes but not Croyle. "You know it was really just a blur," he said. "I probably feared getting rid of the ball as fast as possible. I think at that age you are so in tune to what you want to get to [that] it really doesn't seem that overwhelming. I think the older you get, the more you think of the magnitude of the situation. If they think I'm good enough to do something, then I'm good enough. Of course, I think we went .500 that year. I threw as many interceptions as touchdowns, which is never a good thing. I always remember my dad telling me, 'I don't care what happens, don't care if you have a good game or bad game. My cardinal rule: get up, just get up.' Those words were just always in my ear my whole life. He said, 'If you don't get up, your season is over one way or the other. We understand each other?'

"I played with that mentality. If you go back, there was never a time I didn't get up even when I would have season-ending injuries, and doctors were telling me to stay down. I thought it was more of a Bear Bryant mentality, just having toughness. Never let them see you hurt. It was later on in life I find out my mother was scared to death of me playing varsity football that eighth grade season. He didn't want my mom down there taking me off the field if something were to happen to me. I lived my whole life with this mantra to always get up. Then he ruins it for me. That's really what I remembered most about that eighth grade year."

The 1997 year was a special one for Westbrook. It was an 8–2 season, and the Warriors made an incredible run in the playoffs to advance to its first state championship game led by Croyle and star wide receiver and Alabama signee Brandon Greer. Croyle dislocated his elbow during the season, which he jokingly says is the first picture of what his life and career would be like. The Warriors lost to Billingsley High School in the state title game, but plenty of people started taking notice of the young quarterback from Rainbow City. "I started to get some positive feedback," he said. "Coach Tommy Bowden [at Tulane] offered me when I attended the Bowden Academy. I remember him telling my dad, 'Just remember I was the first one to offer him.' Then, we really opened up the offense. We just ripped it 50 times a game. I had a big year, and that's when everyone started offering me. I can't remember if my first big offer was Alabama, Auburn, or Florida State. It was one of those schools, but once the first one came in, all of them came really at the same time. I liked Alabama, Florida State, Oklahoma, and LSU. Oklahoma ran a similar offense and just won the national championship when I was a junior. They were legit. LSU had Coach Saban as the head coach and Jimbo Fisher. I really liked those guys. Coach Fisher just made you believe you were going to win the Heisman and a national championship. I looked at Miami a little bit but never really considered them. In the end it came down to Alabama and Florida State."

Croyle may not have considered the Hurricanes, but he'll never forget his trip to Coral Gables, Florida, for the Miami–Florida State game, in which an Oklahoma booster would have a surprise in store for him. "The thing that stood out to me more than anything was when I was down at Miami," he said. "They beat Florida State on a last-second field goal. They give you a host for the game. She said to me, 'Is that for you?' I said, 'What's that?' She pointed up. There was a plane flying above the stadium with a sign flying from the back like you see at the beach. It said, 'OU Sooners love Brodie Croyle.'

She didn't know if I was a highly-rated recruit. She thought I was just some skinny kid from Alabama. She probably just thought I was some bum at first. I was just like, 'I guess so.'"

The weight of the world typically causes a lot of anxiety on a player of Croyle's magnitude, and this was prior to the proliferation of recruiting websites and social media. He knew people in Gadsden/Rainbow City wanted him to attend Alabama—at least the Alabama fans. He never let it bother him. "I didn't really ever feel any pressure of being a top recruit," he said. "I can tell you growing up in a fish bowl like I did you can only control what you can control. You can't control the narrative beyond that. I just always put in the work. I threw the ball with conviction and was willing to deal with the consequences that comes with it. That's honestly the mind-set that's always been there. It's playing at a 1A school and wanting to play at a higher level. You are competing against yourself. It may have looked great throwing 17-of-24 for 350 yards and three touchdowns, but why did I miss those seven throws? Why didn't I throw seven touchdown passes? What could I have done better? I'd go home at night. I'd make my dad go to the gym with me, and we'd go over plays and try to figure out why I missed those throws. It can wear you down—even going to Alabama with the hype and expectation. I was aiming for a lot higher. I was young and confident enough to believe it was all going to happen. People were like, 'Man you are going to start as a freshman.' In my mind I'm thinking, *Yeah, and we are going to win a national championship.* Whatever the expectation may have been, I always had one more step beyond it…I was always striving for something more."

Mark Richt, the former Georgia head coach, Miami head coach, and Florida State quarterback coach/offensive coordinator was heavily involved in recruiting Croyle for the Seminoles. Was there a difference in recruiting a small-school star versus a higher classification player? "Not really," Coach Richt said. "Some shy away from small school kids, but I didn't. You can see their fundamentals and skillset. I had some experience with that. Danny Kanell played for me at Florida State. He was from a small school, Westminster Academy, and did very well. I wasn't ever afraid of small school kids."

Ronnie Cottrell, former Alabama assistant head coach and recruiting coordinator and the current head coach of Mobile Christian High School, remembers how easy it was to evaluate Croyle. "Even as a younger player, had a phenomenal release," Cottrell said. "He had a very live arm. He was a three-play evaluation. It took really no time to watch his tape and realize he was going to be a special player. What then really sold you on him was how good of a person he was. He came from a great family. I recruited all kind of kids when I was at Florida State. He was as good as any player I ever recruited. He had great leadership skills. He was a very humble guy. He dominated that level of play, and you just knew he was destined for greatness."

In the 1990s under Bobby Bowden, Florida State was very similar to Coach Saban's program from 2008 to its current run and Coach Bryant in the '70s. The Seminoles won a pair national championships and were considered by many as the team of the decade as it compiled a record of 109–13–1 between 1990 and 1999.

Richt orchestrated the offense in Tallahassee and coached two Heisman winning quarterbacks: Charlie Ward and Chris Weinke. "Coach Richt is still one of my favorite people on this Earth," Croyle said. "He is an incredible man. He has the same heart as my family. They've adopted kids and loved kids who just needed an opportunity. Coach Richt was very influential in my decision. We understood what was coming down the pipeline. We knew he probably wasn't going to be at Florida State the whole time I was there. So we knew going to Florida State because of him would not be the deciding point, but ultimately it did become a major factor."

Richt has three factors when evaluating quarterbacks: accuracy, decision-making, and ability to handle pressure. Croyle checked all of the boxes. "I saw him throw in person and really liked his mechanics," Richt said. "I thought he was very accurate and thought he had good fundamentals. He was a very good athlete and a smart kid. I really thought he could handle the job. I thought he was a really good player."

Coach Richt understood the pressure on Croyle but also never thought his family steered him in any direction. In fact, Florida State was in the driver's seat to land his signature prior to Richt's departure to become the head coach in Athens, Georgia. "I remember being at his house," he said. "Of course, his father, John, was a great player at Alabama and an All-American. He had the Big Oak Ranch. I know a lot of Alabama people were supporting it. I remember his dad saying, 'You will go wherever you want to go. This place will be fine.' He didn't want Brodie to feel like he had to go to Alabama because of that. There was a time when he wanted to go to Florida State. He told me he was coming. The family knew, and I believe they were in the process of telling schools 'thank you for recruiting me.' I don't think he told schools where he was going. He was just telling them he wasn't going to their school.

"I think Alabama caught wind of it, and his phone just started ringing off the hook. You could feel the pressure of him not choosing Alabama while I was in the home. His mother asked me. She said, 'I can't expect you to be [at Florida State] four or five years, but can you promise me you will be there for one year?' I told her, 'I can't promise you that.' I had not come to an agreement with Georgia at that time. I had interviewed with Georgia, Virginia, and a few others. I wouldn't have been in their home that night recruiting Brodie if I knew I was going to Georgia or anywhere else. I knew people were at least contacting me about these jobs. Once I told them I couldn't promise I would be there one year, they kind of said, 'Well, let's make this a soft commitment.' I think it really killed the deal for Florida State. I wasn't going to lie to them. I didn't know if I was going to leave. I had turned down jobs for the last five years and stayed at Florida State."

Alabama started recruiting Croyle during the sophomore season of high school with Cottrell leading the charge as his area recruiter. He also remained in regular contact with head coach Mike DuBose. "People always ask me why I picked No. 12. *Was it because of Namath, Stabler?*" Croyle, who wore No. 5 throughout high school, said. "Oh no, I don't think I had a choice. When Alabama started writing me letters during my sophomore year, they would always put No. 12 on the front of every letter, every single time. They would always say they wanted me to start seeing myself as the next Namath, as the next Stabler, the next great quarterback at Alabama. I don't know if I ever had a choice. I went on my official visit. They had a No. 12 jersey there with my name on the back of it. It was a cool moment because you are out there in the stadium by yourself with the lights. No. 12 was picked for me before I even committed to Alabama."

Croyle's recruitment became intense in the last few months leading up to his December announcement. He was graduating early. He wanted to jump-start his career in college. He was always looking ahead, never looking back. His father, John, knew things would get a little crazy, but some fans are true to the core. "We had one guy who was a big supporter of the ranch tell me, 'If your son doesn't go to Alabama, we will never give you another penny.' I heard that more than once," John said. "The love and loyalty runs deep. I never told Brodie what I thought he should do. He was recruited by the top teams during that time. He had basically committed to go to Florida State."

Brodie never felt pressure to stay in state and go to his father's alma mater despite the immense pressure from the outside world to follow in his footsteps. "My family was great through the whole thing," Croyle said. "They never pressured me in any form or fashion. They did the same thing with the ranch. It's a great life lesson. If we point our kids in the right directions, give them sound counsel and wisdom without giving our opinion, it usually goes the right way. I know they wanted me to go to Alabama. I know they wanted me to come back to the ranch one day, but they never said, 'This is what we see you doing.' I am eternally grateful for them."

DuBose was named the head coach at Alabama after Gene Stallings retired after the 1996 season. DuBose had only one winning season, which was in 1999 and included an SEC championship. Alabama had a disastrous 2000 season, which had lofty expectations prior to its season-opening loss to UCLA. Coach DuBose tendered his resignation after a home loss to UCF, and the Tide finished the regular season 3–8. NCAA sanctions were also looming because of the recruitment of Albert Means. Alabama's sanctions did not happen until a year after Croyle signed with Alabama, but it was a key topic of conversation. Alabama was hit with a two-year bowl ban in 2002, a loss of 21 scholarships in a three-year time span, and five years of probation.

Alabama at the time wasn't a sexy pick, according to Croyle or really anyone who followed college football at the time. Florida State had all the bells and whistles. It was churning out players to the NFL and competing for national championships. Alabama was a long way from doing that. However, Bobby Bowden's in-home visit with the Croyle family prior to Croyle's announcement changed every-thing. "What I remember the most is Coach Bowden coming to my house one of the last days before I was set to make my announce-ment," Croyle said. "We were sitting there having dinner. He is talking to me. I said, 'Coach Bowden, you have done a lot, and I'm leaning heavily toward coming to Florida State.' I said, 'If I come there, will you be there?' It was a big turning point, and I didn't even realize it at the time. He said, 'Son, head coaches come and go. You go to a university because you want to put your name on it. You want to be forever tied to it. That's why you go to that school.'

"I know he was using it as a recruiting pitch, but I always wanted to go to the University of Alabama. I knew it wasn't the greatest situ-ation. They were probably going on probation. They didn't have the ideal coach for my skillset, but that's really where I always dreamed of going. You don't go to a school because of a head coach. How prophetic was that? I signed with Franchione, I practiced with Price, and I finished my career with Shula."

Croyle still has a lot of love for Bowden. "I saw Coach Bowden at Joe Namath's golf tournament," he said. "I was still in the NFL at the time. I had not talked to him since the night he was at my house. So it had been several years. I saw him and said, 'Hey, Coach.' He said, 'Brodie Croyle, Rainbow City. Your mamma still make that good spaghetti?' He remembers all those types of things. That's what made him such a great recruiter. I know he won my mother over after that."

Still, Croyle was not certain of what he was going to do even the night prior to announcing his decision. Alabama hired Dennis

Franchione, a coach he did not know much about other than he typically had an option quarterback. Croyle was a gunslinger. He wanted to rifle the ball to his targets. But Coach Richt and Bowden could not commit to staying at Florida State. "There was really nothing about Coach Fran or his offense that jived with my skill-set," Croyle said. "It goes back to Coach Bowden. It doesn't really matter. Go where you want your name to be tied to the rest of your life. I really didn't know where I was going the night before the announcement. I was leaning toward Alabama because of Coach Bowden's words. My family and I woke up that morning. We met with Coach Fran and Coach Koenning [the offensive coordinator from 2001 to 2002] in Tuscaloosa. I told them: 'If I come in, I'm not an option quarterback. Just show me some guys who he has coached who have had good passing seasons.' We left the meeting. We went by the Bama bookstore on the strip, bought a hat, and then went back to Westbrook for the announcement. I was very grateful for Coach Richt and Coach Bowden. I know Coach Bowden told me those words as a sales pitch for Florida State, but it pointed me in a direction that I don't regret for a single day…I did something I always dreamed of. The coaches, the probation, the circumstances, the lean years in scholarships—none of that matters. What do you want to tie your name to the rest of your life? I wanted to tie mine to the University of Alabama.

"I loved my time at Alabama. I loved the group I did it with. Did we win a national championship? No. Did we get to take pride in being that group that went to Alabama when they weren't the sexy pick? It was something we all believed in. It could have been a really bad time at Alabama. We were part of steadying the ship and getting it pointed in the right direction by the time we got there. DeMeco,

Roman, J.B, those guys I came in with. Would it have been fun to play for Coach Saban? Absolutely, but we grew tremendously."

Croyle redshirted during his freshman season and served as a backup to senior quarterback Tyler Watts in his second season. Franchione resigned to become the head coach at Texas A&M after the Tide's crippling sanctions. Then Mike Price was quickly dismissed after a strip club escapade the following spring. Despite suffering a separated shoulder and two cracked ribs during the season, Croyle started all 11 games as redshirt sophomore under first-year head coach Mike Shula. Alabama finished 3–8. Croyle was off to an incredible start as junior with 534 yards passing and six touchdowns before tearing his ACL in Week Three against Western Carolina.

He had a fully, healthy season as a senior in 2005. It was his best season, and he threw for 2,499 yards passing with 14 touchdowns and only four interceptions. He was named the MVP of the Cotton Bowl against Texas Tech. He was also a finalist for the Johnny Unitas Golden Arm award given to the nation's best senior quarterback.

His father passed on the opportunity to play in the NFL, but Brodie spent five years playing at the highest level with the Kansas City Chiefs and Arizona Cardinals. Injuries, including another torn ACL, plagued his pro career, and he officially retired in 2012. He now runs the Big Oak Ranch, something he never envisioned once he retired from the NFL. "He had the skills to further his career," his father said. "He played in the NFL for five years. It didn't turn out the way he wanted it to, but you know what? A lot of guys who went up there never made it. He played five years. He started. I remember his first game as a starter. He was playing against Peyton Manning and the Indianapolis Colts. I told him, 'There are only 32 men doing what you are doing right now.' He said he never thought about it like that. Starting in an NFL game is a pretty good deal. He had a good career, came back home, and took my job. Brodie is really much better than I was with what he's doing at the ranch. He makes sure to tell me that every week. You know how he is. He does not let any opening go by without firing a shot. He's good at it. He has the heart and passion for it."

CHAPTER 13

DeMeco Ryans

The former SEC Defensive Player of the Year and unanimous first-team All-American linebacker didn't play football during his younger years because he was afraid to get hit. Ryans' first love came from playing on the offensive side of the ball rather than defense. Alabama fans can also thank a star from the rival school for the advice he gave to the future All-Pro, which helped steer him to the Crimson Tide.

Ryans grew up in Bessemer, Alabama, just outside of Birmingham. He was the youngest of four children. His older siblings were Travis Head, Serena Head Watkins, and Lodist Ryans. He was raised by a hard-working, God-fearing single parent in Martha Ryans. His father, Morgan Turner, lived in Birmingham, but Ryans lived with his mother. His mom spent 12 years at Southern Ductile Casting Corp. making car parts and often worked a second job in cleaning services. "I had to work most of the time, but to have all my kids around was very exciting," Martha said. "I worked two or three jobs. I thought my kids were okay while I was working. They always did what I said to do. They stayed in the house. I left them food, and they would warm it up. It was definitely a challenge at times. They were always playing sports. One thing they always wanted to do before they came home every night was go to McDonald's. It didn't matter if there was food at home. They go to McDonald's then come home and eat the food that was at home."

DeMeco loved baseball growing up but football—not so much. Football is a way of life in Alabama, especially for kids in the Birmingham area. There are plenty of peewee and youth teams. Most of DeMeco's friends played football at a young age. He had zero interest because he didn't want to get tackled. "My older cousins played football, and my brother played a little," DeMeco said. "Everyone played Little League football where I was from. I really just loved playing baseball. I would always go to my grandparents' house. They always had a Braves or Cubs game on. I started playing baseball when I was six years old. My mom would take me out for football every year, but I would see guys get hit and think, *I don't want to play football.* I was scared to play. I wouldn't even get out of the van. I would always just say, 'Maybe next year.' All my buddies played football, and they always talked about it."

But his Little League baseball coach convinced Ryans to play football. "I went out my eighth grade year," he said. "It's extremely late for someone to go out that late around here. I really didn't even know what position I would play. I'm still out there scared for my life. I remember this one drill where they had two guys lay down on their back, the coach blows the whistle, and you get up to hit each other…I was still trying to find my way. I stood on the sideline, watching practice for the most part. I kept seeing the quarterback and center working together. They kept fumbling the snap. I looked at them and said I think I can do that. I ended up playing center and started during my eighth grade year. I was out there playing and getting used to it. If you want to survive in football, you have to hit the guy you are going up against first. When I was playing center, I always had to go out and block the middle linebacker. When I started blocking the linebacker, I started thinking I wanted to play linebacker. Our top player was suspended the first half of a game. I told the coaches I can play linebacker. I played both ways that night. I literally made every tackle in the first half."

His mom didn't mind him playing football. She wanted him to do whatever he wanted as long as he was staying out of trouble, which was never much of an issue. "He was very quiet," she said. "He was just a good child. He never got any whoopin's. The kids above him took a bunch of whoppin's. He didn't want that. He was very obedient. He was very smart. He always brought home A's in school. He did his lessons and what teachers told him to do. Something changed during his eighth-grade year. He never wanted to be hit. I didn't mind if he played football. I was always going to support him and attend his games in whatever he decided to do. I know he was playing baseball. I really wanted him to play baseball, but it didn't matter to me if he played football."

Ryans knew when he moved to high school his days of playing on the offensive line had reached its end. "I remember when we were freshmen, and the coach said, 'Who was the center last year?'" Ryans said. "Of course, some of my buddies said, 'Meco.' I didn't want to play center anymore. He put me down for center, but then I went and ran the 40. He said, 'Okay, I want you to play with the running backs.' I ended up playing on the freshman team as a linebacker. I really didn't understand how good I was. Our freshman season ended, and I was at home just playing around. I got a call asking why I wasn't at practice. They told me I was on the varsity team now. Just getting that experience as a freshman playing with the varsity guys was great for me. My linebacker career kind of took off from there."

Jess Lanier High School was coached by Alabama Sports Hall of Famer Carroll Cox between 1973 and 2000. He served as the team's head football coach and athletic director for 21 years before he retired. After Coach Cox hung up his whistle, it was a struggle during Ryans' junior season as the Purple Tigers finished 1–9 under first-year head coach Willie Ford. Things did not get much better after the 2000 season. Ryans expected a big turnaround during his final season. He was receiving recruiting attention from small schools but wanted to go out on a high note and hopefully attract attention from SEC programs, including Alabama. "Things really took off during my senior year," he said. "I had an assistant coach, Ty Lockett, come in that year. He was a younger guy. He had just finished playing linebacker at Alabama State. He really taught me how to read linemen. He taught me real techniques and fundamentals of playing the linebacker position. He really helped take my game to another level. It really helped me catch the eye of some big colleges."

Lanier finished with a 9–3 record. The team lost to Hoover High in the season opener 14–12 and to Tuscaloosa County 21–6 during the regular season. Tuscaloosa County featured a pair of his future teammates in running back Le'Ron McClain and linebacker Terrence Jones. Both were in the 2003 recruiting class. Jess Lanier made it to the third round of the Class 6A playoffs but got knocked out 28–17 by Hoover, which had a sophomore quarterback, John Parker Wilson, who replaced senior quarterback Blake Davidson when the starter went down with an injury the previous week.

Ryans' performance throughout his senior season earned him Super All-Star honors and an invitation to the Alabama/Mississippi

All-Star Classic. Ryans finished his high school senior season with 135 tackles, 11 sacks, two forced fumbles, and two interceptions. "He was remarkable," Lockett said. "He made my job easy. I was a young guy, just out of college. It was my second year out of college. The most amazing thing is he allowed me to coach him. He actually took the things I gave him and put them into his game. I didn't do a whole lot. I just gave him a few nuggets that I learned when I played. It helped take his game to another level. It was one of the easiest jobs I ever had. He was really cerebral. He understood the game. He understood how the offense and defense worked. A lot of high school players don't understand schemes. I was just so impressed with how well he understood the game. We could talk football at a high level. I didn't have to break down things for him to understand. I'm not surprised with what he's done. He was a humble guy. He worked hard. I was not surprised by anything he has accomplished."

Recruiting letters poured in for Ryans during his senior season. He wasn't a five-star guy and did not have a plethora of SEC programs banging on the door for his commitment. (Rivals.com gave him three stars.) There were only a few schools he expected to choose from late in the recruiting process: Ole Miss, Southern Miss, or UAB. "Alabama kind of came on late in the process," he said. "Once Bama came around though...Growing up in Alabama football is really a way of life. So you are taught at an early age to choose between Alabama and Auburn. Most of my family were Auburn fans. They all liked Auburn because of Bo Jackson because he is from Bessemer. All my uncles were big Auburn fans, really everyone in my family. I chose to be an Alabama fan just to be different from everyone else. Alabama came in and offered me. I'm thinking I have this huge opportunity now to go to Alabama."

On January 12, 2002, a few weeks from Signing Day, Ryans took an official visit to Alabama. His mother said she was treated "like royalty" throughout the weekend. DeMeco remembers it like it was yesterday. "Alabama offered me during my official visit," he said. "Coach Franchione came up to me on that Saturday night and offered me. It was a weird time because there were limited scholarships [because of NCAA sanctions.] I think there were only 16 scholarship players that year. They offered me, and I was just speechless. I spoke to Alabama defensive coordinator Carl Torbush the next morning. He sold me on coming to Alabama regardless of everything that was going on. I committed on that Sunday during the official visit. It was a done deal. Coach Stan Eggen was the one who recruited me for Alabama. The biggest thing about Alabama is the tradition. Alabama was the staple program. That was the team growing up. I knew the history of Alabama football. I remember going there as a young boy and then going back for my official. I just had that same feeling when I was there each time. I walked around and felt at home."

He never thought someone who attended that rival school and became a Heisman Trophy winner from Auburn would help him reach that college decision. "Pat Sullivan was at UAB at the time," Ryans said. "He was recruiting me and gave me a little advice about the recruiting process. He said, 'Nobody will be able to tell you where to go. You will just know. You are going to know within yourself. It's just like when you get married to your wife. You're going to know.' I remember Pat Sullivan giving me those words of advice. When I went on Alabama's campus, I immediately felt like I was home. There were other guys on the team like Todd Bates, Freddie Roach, and Brandon Brooks, who showed me around and took me under their wing. It was just a family-type atmosphere from the start. I have to give big credit to those guys for making me feel very special."

Martha Ryans enjoyed getting to know various coaches throughout her son's recruitment. She'll never forget the trip to UAB when coaches asked if she was DeMeco's sister instead of his mother. She also loved watching fans come up to him after games for his autograph. It warmed her heart to see different people from all walks of life wanting her son's signature. "There were so many letters from so many esteemed colleges," she said, "just a lot of great schools from Yale to Alabama. It shocked me. Guys at the plant kept saying he was going to make it. It was exciting. We didn't have anyone in our family go to Alabama. It was really exciting for him to go down there. I was so happy with all the opportunities he could get involved in. Everyone in our family was big Auburn fans. I stayed true to my son. I was excited, knowing he would be close to home. I thought he would come home more often, but I was dead wrong about that. He didn't come home too much when he got to Alabama. I went down there as much as I could. I was at every game."

Ryans continued to play baseball throughout high school. He was a catcher, but his future was in football much like former Jess Lanier stars Kerry Rhodes and Earl Cochran, who had made it to the NFL. He knew he could earn a scholarship after watching the guys before him. But the dream could have been crushed after his freshman season at Alabama when Dennis Franchione left Tuscaloosa to become the head coach at Texas A&M. "It was weird," Ryans said. "I was a young freshman hearing all these rumors of Coach Fran leaving. Of course, he was telling us he wasn't going anywhere. Then we had this weird meeting about Coach Fran leaving us. As a young freshman, you don't know what to think, but I was committed to being a part of the University of Alabama. I was with my family, those guys in the locker room. Those are Alabama guys. I didn't feel like I was losing anything besides a head coach. I still had my family at Alabama, the guys who were on the team. It didn't change anything."

Coach Franchione left Alabama in December of 2002. Alabama hired Washington State head coach Mike Price after he took Washington State to the Rose Bowl. Price remained in Tuscaloosa throughout the spring until his contract was rescinded in May after reports emerged of his infamous strip club trip in Pensacola, Florida, and various reports of late nights in local watering holes in Tuscaloosa. Alabama hired former alum and quarterback, Mike Shula, to replace Price. Shula had been an assistant coach in the NFL for several seasons and accepted his first head coaching job with the Crimson Tide at 38 years old. He is also the son of Hall of Fame coach Don Shula, the winningest football coach in NFL history.

Ryans became the first in his family to go to a four-year college and graduate. He was one of only two true freshmen to see the field for the Tide in 2002. Alabama finished the season 10–3 and in first place in the SEC West, but due to sanctions, the Tide were not allowed to participate in postseason games, including the SEC Championship Game.

He led the team in tackles during his sophomore season with 126 and had an amazing 25 tackles against Arkansas in Coach Shula's first season with the Tide, but Alabama only had a 4–9 record. Ryans had 78 tackles during his junior season, including seven tackles for loss. Alabama was invited to the Music City Bowl after a 6–5 season but lost to Minnesota. Alabama had a tremendous 2005 season and finished 10–2, including a Cotton Bowl victory, in which Ryans was named MVP. Ryans led the team in tackles (76) and had 9.5 tackles for loss during that senior season.

Ryans was a unanimous first-team All-American and first-team All-SEC in 2005. He was also named SEC Defensive Player of the Year. He was awarded the Lott Trophy after his senior season for his combination of athletic excellence and off-the-field achievement. Ryans currently ranks fifth all time in career tackles (309), second in a single-season tackles (126), and second in tackles in a single game (25) at Alabama. Ryans was also a three-time Academic All-SEC selection.

Ryans graduated cum laude (3.55 GPA) with a bachelor's degree in business marketing in only seven semesters. He was awarded the NCAA's Top VIII Award, recognizing outstanding achievement in athletics, scholarship, and community service. The award is given annually to only eight student-athletes nationwide.

After being drafted No. 33 overall in the second round by the Houston Texans in 2006, he was named the AP Defensive Rookie of the Year in 2006 and recorded 156 tackles. He was named first-team All-Pro and earned two invites to the Pro Bowl (2007 and 2009). He registered 735 tackles, 46 passes defended, 13.5 sacks, 10 fumble recoveries, and seven interceptions during his NFL career. He was traded to the Philadelphia Eagles in 2012. He played four seasons with the Eagles before retiring from the NFL in 2016. Ryans currently coaches linebackers for the San Francisco 49ers. He and his wife, Jamila, have two boys: MJ and Micah and one daughter: Xia.

Ryans credits his defensive coordinator in Tuscaloosa for helping him have such a successful career in football. "I'd say the person who had the biggest impact on me, as far as college, is Joe Kines," Ryans said. "Joe taught us not only about football but about life, just the simple things. He told us: 'always put a suit on when we were going to football games because it was a business trip. One day, you'll be going on a real business trip.' He always let me call the plays. He'd always ask me in the meeting rooms while we were watching film what play I would call in different situations. I look back on it now as a coach. He was getting me ready for the position I'm in now. I think back to those days and just think about how much of an impact Coach Kines had on my life."

Of course, Martha had the most influence upon his life. "My mother was also so significant in my life with the impact she had," he said. "I saw the work she put in every day. She has worked two-or-three jobs just to put food on the table and always provide for us. It showed me if you want anything in life, you have to work hard at it to be successful. We went to church every week, pretty much every day it was open. I'm really appreciative of my mom doing that—now that I'm an adult. Church, family, and sports was a really big deal to us. I know it was tough for her living paycheck to paycheck, but she always made sure to take care of us. I never missed a meal, but I know it was rough."

Ryans pledged $300,000 in 2011 to endow a full scholarship in his name for a deserving football student-athlete studying in the Alabama's Culverhouse College of Commerce and Business Administration. He also established the DeMeco Ryans Foundation in Bessemer, which helps create innovative programs that provide access to educational, recreational, and healthy living initiatives designed to positively aid in the development of youth.

Doing the right thing was instilled in Ryans. He set a great example when he stood up in a team meeting four days after Hurricane Katrina and announced he would donate his $27 per diem for the game to the American Red Cross. The entire team followed his lead. Coach Shula matched the total. "A lot of people think when you get a scholarship, that that's it," Martha said. "A lot of guys still need money to survive in college. They still need money. Some of the boys get in trouble for selling books. People don't realize they need the extra cash. I was always very proud of Meco [for] giving back to Alabama for all they did for us. I was really proud when he made it. I was proud when he made it to college. So many of them don't. They get into trouble. I kept him in church. It really thrilled my heart when he wanted to go to college. He always wanted to be something in life. He would always tell me, 'I'm going to put Bessemer on the map.' I think he did a great job."

CHAPTER 14

Barrett Jones

A basketball coach and one of the world's most powerful sports agents had an indirect way of helping Alabama land one of the most decorated offensive linemen in its rich history. Barrett Jones was part of Nick Saban's first No. 1 recruiting class at Alabama in 2008. The class featured the likes of Heisman Trophy winner Mark Ingram, Julio Jones, Mark Barron, Marcell Dareus, Terrence Cody, Dont'a Hightower, and Courtney Upshaw. Jones was part of something special in Tuscaloosa during his career. After winning his first national championship at Alabama, Saban said, "This is not the end. This is the beginning."

Basketball has always run deep in the Jones family. His father, Rex, moved to Florence, Alabama, when he was 12 years old and is the son of Bill Jones, the head basketball coach and athletic director at the University of North Alabama from 1974 to 1988. North Alabama made it to four NCAA Division II Final Fours during that time span and won the national championship in 1979. Rex's father was also inducted into the Alabama Sports Hall of Fame in 2013. "Every summer C.M. Newton had a basketball camp in Florence," Rex Jones said. "That's where I ignited my love for Alabama. He started recruiting me in the eighth grade. My lifelong goal was to play at Alabama."

Rex signed with Alabama in 1981 with then-head coach Wimp Sanderson. He was part of a recruiting class, which featured NBA first-round draft pick Ennis Whatley and Bobby Lee Hurt, who is the all-time leader in field goal percentage for the Tide. Rex met his wife, Leslie, in high school, but she attended North Alabama, where his father coached instead of following him to Tuscaloosa. Both graduated on the same day in May of 1985 and married the next month. Rex had plans to attend the University of Tennessee dental school but instead decided to work with his father-in-law and run businesses, which included car dealerships in Memphis, Tennessee, and Little Rock, Arkansas.

Barrett was born on May 25, 1990. He also has two younger brothers who played at Alabama: Harrison and Walker. "My kids all grew at different stages," Rex said. "I had a rule where you couldn't play organized football until sixth grade. I played one year in sixth grade. I wanted them to grow a little bit before they played padded football. Barrett was like a Great Dane. He was a baby puppy who had big legs and big feet. He just couldn't get his feet up under him. He played in the church basketball league. He was the kid who didn't score all season. He was uncoordinated, long-legged kid. I told his mom one day, 'I was really glad he played the violin because he will never be able to make the football team.'"

Barrett wanted to try out for the football team after a few rough years playing basketball. He may not have been great when he first started, but he was in the development stage, and his body soon caught up to him. "I was always tall, but I wasn't really a good athlete," Jones said. "I went a whole season in third grade as the tallest kid in the league and did not score a single basket. My coordination finally caught up with my height in middle school. I started being able to move pretty good.

"I remember my first football game. I was on the sixth and seventh grade team. I was one of the only sixth grade starters. We got killed like 34–0. My parents thought I was going to hate it. I walked back to the car after the game ended and told them I was born to play football. I loved this sport. I told them it was awesome. I had such a fun time out there, even though we lost. I was playing linebacker. I had a blast. I really loved it from the get-go. I loved the team aspect of it all and the physicality. It was just really fun to play."

Jones attended Evangelical Christian School in Memphis from kindergarten through high school. He continued to show improvement every year in middle school from an athletic standpoint and competed against another famous lineman from Memphis. "When I got to high school as a freshman, I played exclusively at defensive end," he said. "I played a little bit, but I wasn't starting. Our starter at the time went down in the state championship. I went in and went up against Michael Oher, the same one from the movie, *The Blind Side*. That was a rude awakening. I was 6'5", 210 pounds at the time. He was 6'5", 340 pounds. I felt like I held my own against him. He got me a few times. I don't know if I ever got him, but I know I hung in there. I started on the offensive line at left tackle as a sophomore. I played offensive line and defensive line during my junior and senior seasons. I was always a left tackle."

Jones made a significant leap once he became a full-time starter. He was hoping to play another position on the offensive side but was only able to showcase those skills during practice. "I remember battling it for a long time," he said. "I was more upset because I really wanted to be a tight end. Jason Witten was my favorite player. I thought I could go and be a tight end just like him. I used to always beg the coaches to let me run as a tight end. They would only let me do it when the defense was doing their thing at practice. We were really good during my 10th grade season. Our team was stacked, and we won the state championship that year. They didn't need me to go both ways, so I just played on offense. I had a really good year on the offensive line. I finally just embraced it."

Jimmy Sexton of Creative Artists Agency represents former Alabama stars such as Julio Jones and C.J. Mosley. He also represents quarterbacks like Sam Darnold and Philip Rivers. But Sexton is probably better known as the agent to many of the top coaches in college football, including Saban. He is known as Uncle Jimmy to Barrett Jones. Sexton gave Jones, his next-door neighbor, sound advice after his sophomore season. "I went to him one day and asked him, 'How do I know if I can really play at the next level?'" Jones said. "He said, 'You need to sign up for some of these camps.' So I signed up for the Auburn, Tennessee, and Alabama camp that summer. This is right after we won the state championship my sophomore year."

His father remembers the neighbor's conversation and the idea he had in mind if he was not paying college tuition. "Barrett told me one day that he thought there is a chance he may want to play college football," Rex said. "I told him I would make a deal with him. I told him if he gets a scholarship, I would buy him any car he wanted. He said, 'Man I'm going to get a new car.' So he walked over to Jimmy Sexton's house and asked what did he needed to do to get schools to take notice of him. He told him to go to those three camps [Alabama, Auburn, and Tennessee]. I told him I wasn't going to spend time on Auburn's campus. I said if he wanted to go, we would drop him off, go to the beach, and when the camp ended, we would come back and pick him up."

Auburn was coming off its fourth consecutive win against the Tide in the summer of 2006. Jones attended the Tommy Tuberville Football Camp at Auburn. It was the first time he was acknowledged on the recruiting scene. "I did really well in the camp," he said. "You know I'm from a private, medium-sized school. I graduated with about 120 kids. I thought I did pretty good in camp, but this was around the same time as when Rivals.com started to really blow up. It was around before then, but the popularity in recruiting really started around then. I wasn't really familiar with how everything worked. I wasn't on the map as a recruit yet. I lost only one rep in the camp to a guy who was a year older than me, Ian Williams. He went to Notre Dame.

"I remember after the camp they asked me to come meet Coach Tuberville. They said when your parents come to pick you up to bring them to Coach Tuberville's office. I just figured that's what everyone did after the camp. I remember going up there. I shook Coach Tuberville's hand. That was around the time when Auburn had beaten Alabama four times in a row. Everything in his office said, 'Fear the Thumb.' They were really into that.

"I grew up an Alabama fan, but it's not like I hated Auburn. I grew up in Memphis, so I didn't really care too much about the whole rivalry thing, but I did cheer for Alabama against Auburn. I was just more in awe at the time to be in an SEC coach's office. He then offered me a scholarship. I was blown away. I really didn't know until that moment that I could go on to the next level. I started working very hard to be an offensive lineman. I was thinner because I was playing basketball. I was 6'5", 230 pounds the summer before my junior season. I am a very analytical guy. I started thinking, *I am not going to be a defensive end for a major college. I'm never going to be an All-American defensive end.* It's all about body type. Offensive line is where I fit the best. I still played defensive end for the next two seasons, but I really focused on becoming a great offensive lineman."

His father wasn't sure what was happening in Auburn. He certainly didn't expect a scholarship offer to take place. "The day before we went to pick him up, Barrett called and said, 'Y'all need to come about an hour early because Coach Tuberville wants to talk to you.' I said, 'Barrett what did you do? Did you get in trouble?' He said, 'No they just want to talk to you about my camp.' I seriously thought he just did that with every kid who went through the camp," Rex said. "We went up there an hour early, and he offered Barrett a scholarship. I was in shock. Barrett is in shock. I'm thinking to myself, *What have we gotten ourselves into?* That's where it all started. People found out he got an offer from Auburn. Pretty much after that, he was offered by everyone in the country once the news started to spread."

Alabama is one of the few programs who did not extend an immediate offer even after Jones camped in Tuscaloosa. Maybe Mike Shula thought he could wait because of his friendship with Rex during their college days together at Alabama. It wasn't until Coach Shula was fired and Saban was hired that Alabama became seriously interested. It was almost immediately after Jones' junior season when he spoke with Coach Saban. "I remember going to Alabama's camp, and it really didn't go that well," Jones said. "Coach Shula was still there. It was fine, but I wanted to win. That was a priority for me along with a free education and going to a school I loved. I wanted to go to a program I felt would be competitive. I didn't get a great sense from Alabama in that regard. They were really the only school who didn't offer me right away. They were slow-playing me, but I was already thinking I was probably not going to go there. I didn't really care that much. I was just more impressed with other schools I was visiting at the time. The recruiting hype really picked up after my junior season.

"Coach Saban arrived and pretty much as soon as he got there he contacted me. Alabama really came back into the picture for me when Coach Saban got there. I knew Jimmy, who is like an uncle to me, really liked Coach Saban. I went with him to some games and was down on the sideline when Coach Saban was at LSU. I was always impressed with Coach Saban."

Georgia Tech head coach Geoff Collins remembers evaluating Jones when he was the director of player personnel at Alabama in 2007 during Coach Saban's first season with the Crimson Tide. "Barrett was big, physical, and had very good flexibility," Coach Collins said. "He was also an unbelievable person once you met him and talked to him. Just a great guy and great family. He had a great upbringing. Then you turn the tape on. He had that physical and nasty demeanor and then finished plays until the whistle blows. A lot of the time, you don't get both of those together; Barrett had both. I remember he also took some reps at tight end. He also had some versatility to go along with his athletic ability."

Former Alabama defensive coordinator Kevin Steele (currently the defensive coordinator at Auburn University) also remembered the immediate attention paid to Jones upon their arrival as a coaching staff at Alabama. Coach Steele led the Tide's recruiting charge for the future two-time consensus All-American lineman. "It was a different situation because we were a new staff," Coach Steele said. "I knew Rex and Leslie before I came to Alabama. We knew Barrett was going to be a big guy and be a good player. He played basketball.

He was intelligent and had a strong work ethic. When we first got to Alabama, the name came up, and I knew about him. Coach Saban, coming from the NFL, quickly knew about him because of Jimmy Sexton. A lot of people in the Sexton tree would ask Jimmy about Barrett. He had a pretty big explosion in recruiting. It wasn't abnormal, but it grew pretty fast. Not because of Jimmy, but he was able to help get his video out there and into the right hands."

Jones was a heavily-recruited prospect prior to the start of his senior season. He took several visits including Alabama, Auburn, Florida, North Carolina, Stanford, and Tennessee. When it came time to figure out real schools in the race for his signature, it was between the Crimson Tide, Gators, and, surprisingly, the Tar Heels. "I really liked Florida a lot," he said. "They had Tim Tebow and Urban Meyer at the time. I thought Florida was a really cool place. Steve Addazio was the offensive coordinator. I loved him. I thought he was great. I also really liked North Carolina a lot. Sam Pittman was the offensive line coach at that time. I loved him too and thought he was great. I was also recruited heavily by Stanford. Jim Harbaugh was actually one of the only coaches who was a little mad at me. He thought I was making a huge mistake by going to Alabama. He really gave me the business when I told him I was going to Alabama, but I thought I was making the right move, which I did.

"I always liked Tennessee, but there was a lot of turmoil going on there with Coach Fulmer and the uncertainty of the direction of the program. I liked Auburn a lot at one time. I visited them a few times. I looked at them pretty hard, but for whatever reason, I became more focused on Alabama, North Carolina, and Florida. North Carolina was very much in it. I liked them a lot and was impressed with Butch Davis. I thought they had the program going in the right direction.

They had a lot of really good recruits on board, but then they got caught cheating. Florida was very high on my list. They were really rolling at the time."

Saban was putting together a strong recruiting class in his first full year at the helm in Tuscaloosa. Most assumed the Alabama legacy was a lock to join the Tide's class based on his family connections. But his commitment didn't have anything to do with carrying on the family tradition at the Capstone. "I wasn't that interested in Alabama at the start," Jones said. "I was looking for a combination of things. I wanted to win, I wanted to go to a great school. Coach Saban introduced me to Dr. Witt [the University of Alabama president from 2003 to 2012] along with a lot of people in the business school and honors programs. They rolled out the red carpet for me and showed me how I could challenge myself academically. He set up meetings for me with all the academic people. Dr. Witt was also very impressive. He took me into his office. I am an analytical guy. I wanted to know the ins and outs of being a student at Alabama. I met the right kind of people from FCA to Campus Crusade. Those were things I wanted to be involved in. Plus I liked the fact I could win a lot of games and be in a competitive atmosphere. I also always wanted to play for the same coach. I thought Coach Saban was going to be there for a long time."

There was a point in Jones' recruitment when Steele thought he might go to Tennessee, but he was pretty happy when he learned the Memphis native was headed to Alabama. "It was unusual because Rex being an Alabama graduate and former Alabama basketball player, knowing he loved the University of Alabama, then Leslie, being the kind of mom she is, wanting Barrett to do whatever Barrett decided rather than going to where everyone expected him to go," Coach Steele said. "Barrett is extremely intelligent. With that intelligence is a wisdom where he played everything very, very close to the vest. He was smart enough to know when people were asking questions to extract information to try and figure out what he is going to do, so you could never really get anything out of him. I remember a good while before he announced his decision, he told me privately what he was going to do. I guess people expected him to go to Alabama since his dad graduated from there, but that was not the case at all. He could have easily gone somewhere else. I really think he chose Alabama because of the competitive spirit and the challenge of that spirit that Coach Saban presented to him in recruiting. It was a big day for us the day he committed."

Jones said he wasn't certain about his decision, and that's why he waited late into his senior season before announcing his commitment to Alabama. "I definitely didn't know until after I took my visits," he said. "I was impressed with what Alabama was doing and I could see Coach Saban building the program. I saw a drastic improvement on the field, just the way they were operating. It had very little to do with my dad and fanhood. I felt like it was trending in the right direction and felt good about a lot of other stuff going on in the program. I remember Coach Saban coming to my house for an in-home visit. We had lasagna that night. After dinner we had the longest talk I've ever had with Coach Saban. He talked about the process. Every coach tells you how they are going to turn the program into a winner because of you. I thought I was a really good fit for the process. I really believed Coach Saban when he told me he was going to win. I remember buying in and wanting to be a part of it. He also didn't beg me to come. He challenged me to come to Alabama to compete against the best and become a better player and person. I wanted to be a part of that. I wanted to be part of something special.

"I also have a soft spot for Coach Steele. It's hard to hate Auburn because I love the guy so much. He is a great guy. He understood me. He understood what was important to me. Coach Saban understood that as well. I remember the first time I went to Alabama before Coach Saban was there. It was so unorganized. When I went back, Coach Saban had his handprint on everything in the program. It was so organized, just so many little things. I generally just wanted to see the campus and see the academic stuff. Coach Saban knew that's what I wanted. I had a very positive experience when I took my visit. He paid so much attention to every little detail, and it was an indicator to me how the program would be run. My relationship with Coach Pendry was also very huge. I knew I'd be spending a lot of time with the offensive line coach. It was very important to me to have a good offensive line coach. I knew Coach Pendry had been around for a long time. I knew he was going to make me better. I wasn't looking for a buddy. I knew guys like Coach Saban and Coach Pendry would make me a better player."

His father was a recruit in the early 1980s, and his dream was to play basketball for Alabama. Rex wanted Barrett to carve his own path and was going to guide him rather than lead him to his college destination. "I kept telling him, 'It's not my decision or his mother's decision,'" Rex said. "He is a 16-year old young man. I told him, 'I'll teach you how to make good decisions, but know I'll never tell you where to go to school. My role is to take you to all these places and see them for what they are. You are making the decision based on how it relates to football but also education, and this will shape the rest of your life. That's why we are going to do this the right way.' We really took on this journey. I bought a custom van, and we started taking trips every weekend in the fall. We would drive or fly to every

SEC school. We went to North Carolina. We went to some schools outside the SEC. I think he wanted to play in the SEC. I think after he talked to Coach Saban, he fell in love with Coach Saban and the vision he had for the Alabama program.

"He took a lot of faith on his part to believe in what Coach Saban was saying was true. I'm telling you everything he told Barrett came to fruition. It was incredible to watch how he developed, shaped, and modeled that program and for that long period of time. Barrett was in that first full recruiting class. I still believe to this day there has never been a better recruiting class than 2008. It helped springboard what the program is today.

"He was offered by schools like Stanford, North Carolina, and Vanderbilt. He had a 4.0 average in high school. He was making a business and personal decision. I told him to pray about where God wants you to go. When he did all that and came to the decision he wanted to go to Alabama, we told him we would be behind him 100 percent if that's what God is telling you to do. It was as much of a calling than anything for him to go and experience what he did with Coach Saban and what he teaches. He takes boys and makes them into men. I never asked Coach Saban to be a spiritual mentor, but I did ask for him to teach Barrett to work, to be a good person, good student, and good teammate. Coach Saban committed those things to me and Leslie. From there on out, he did everything he said he was going to do.

"I'll say this: there was a point and time when we had sold our family company. I was working at the high school and was involved in athletics. Coaches would come into my office. It was the who's who coming by the school. I'll always remember I never had one coach ever offer anything illegal or improper. Nobody ever said, 'If

Barrett comes here, we will do this or that.' That was really encouraging to me because I was really dreading that part of it. All the coaches who were recruiting Barrett were above board. I also never forget one thing Coach Saban said to Barrett. He said he could come there and win national championships. Barrett said that's what he wanted to do. He said, 'I can't promise you playing time, but we will compete for championships.' And they did."

With the 2008 recruiting class, Alabama set the bar and helped change the culture of the program. It was the Tide's first No. 1 recruiting class in the Saban era, but it certainly wasn't the last. Alabama finished with the No. 1 recruiting class again in 2009, 2011, 2012, 2013, 2014, 2016, and 2017. It finished with the No. 2 class in 2015 and 2019. Alabama also finished No. 3 in 2020. "Results wise, it's one of the best overall classes in history," Barrett said. "You look at all the different players who were in the class like Julio Jones, Mark Ingram, Mark Barron, Marcell Dareus, Dont'a Hightower, Courtney Upshaw, Terrence Cody, and Damion Square. There were so many good players in that class. A lot of those guys ended up being superstars and great leaders. It was just an awesome class. That class changed the culture of what Alabama was and even what they are today. I thought we had a really good class coming in, but you really don't know because there isn't much to compare it to. You have to wait to see how it all shakes out once you get there. Once we got there as freshmen, doing all the conditioning stuff, and just realizing it's a pretty good group, you could tell it was a changing of the guard. Some of the seniors were very much on board, but some of the older guys were so indoctrinated into a culture that did things differently. We were kind of a clean slate, and I think in some ways it is an advantage. There was certainly some good conflict there with younger guys pushing and taking spots. It wasn't business as usual anymore. You have to earn everything. It was a very competitive atmosphere."

Jones started on the 2009 national championship team at right guard as a redshirt freshman. Alabama defeated Texas in the Rose Bowl for Coach Saban's first title in Tuscaloosa. Jones earned freshman All-American honors. He switched from guard to left tackle during his junior season. He helped Alabama to another national championship with a win against LSU in the Sugar Bowl. He was a unanimous first-team All-American, first-team All-SEC selection, and winner of the Outland Trophy, which is given to the nation's best lineman. Jones also won the Jacobs Blocking Trophy given to the best blocker in the SEC.

He was moved from tackle to center during his redshirt senior season and helped Alabama to a third BCS national championship in a win against Notre Dame in the Orange Bowl. Jones was a consensus All-American and All-SEC selection once again and won the Rimington Trophy given to the most outstanding center in college football. He is the only person to win an Outland Trophy and Rimington Trophy at two different positions or in two different years. He ended his career playing three different positions on three national championship teams.

His academic achievements off the field were also outstanding. He earned a degree in accounting with a 4.0, graduating summa cum laude in August 2011. He graduated with a master's and also got a 4.0 in that program. He was honored in 2011 as one of 11 members of the Allstate AFCA Good Work, which goes to student-athletes for doing exemplary community service work. He is a 2010 and 2011 Academic All-American. In 2012–13 he earned the NCAA Division I Football Academic All-America Team Member of the Year and the

Academic All-American Team Member of the Year for all NCAA Division I sports. He received the 2011 ARA Sportsmanship Award and 2011 Wuerffel Trophy for combined athletic, academic, and community service achievement.

Jones was selected in the fourth round (No. 113 overall) of the NFL draft by the St. Louis Rams in 2013. Jones retired from football after the 2016 season. He was the lead analyst for ESPN Radio during the 2019 season, in which he covered 24 games including the Fiesta, Sugar, and Orange Bowls. He also works as a financial advisor in Memphis.

CHAPTER 15

Trent Richardson

Fans may remember Trent Richardson as a high-profile five-star recruit who had his choice of choosing pretty much any college in the country, but it was not until September 28, 2008, during his senior season at Escambia High School in Pensacola, Florida, when his stock rose to another level. It was the first time I saw Richardson play football in person. He was already committed to the University of Alabama, though schools such as Florida, Florida State, and LSU were still in heavy pursuit. Richardson asked me prior to kickoff, "When are you guys going to make me a five-star?"

He went on to rush for 419 yards that night with six touchdowns on 29 carries against Milton High School. Richardson introduced me to his two-year old daughter, Taliyah, after the game. He followed up by asking, "Am I a five-star now?" Two days later the video I recorded was uploaded, and a five-star ranking was issued to Richardson in the ensuing rankings update.

Richardson admits he wanted the status. He had endured so many hardships from growing up in a rough area in Pensacola to suffering season-ending injuries in back-to-back years in high school. He had attention and he had scholarship offers. He was a regional track champion and state weightlifting champion. He still felt like he was slighted. He talked to NFL Hall of Fame running back Emmitt Smith prior to his 419-yard rushing performance and told him to watch him play. "He said to just go out there and do my thing, show why I'm one of the top running backs in the country," Richardson said.

Smith was a mentor to Richardson throughout his recruitment. The three-time Super Bowl winner, NFL MVP, and member of the Hall of Fame was also a star at Escambia High School before signing with the University of Florida in 1987. Smith is a legend in Pensacola, and Richardson was hoping to create his own legacy. Jimmy Nichols was the offensive coordinator at Escambia when Smith was in high school. He returned as the head coach during Richardson's junior season. "Nichols realized he had Emmitt Smith Part II in Trent," said Dennis Boyd, who served as an assistant coach during Richardson's junior and senior season. He also became Richardson's confidant throughout his recruitment. "Trent was just bigger, faster, and more physical. Coach Nichols used to always say Emmitt had better vision, but Trent had everything else."

Richardson was born on July 10, 1990 and lived in the Warrington Village apartments. He also lived in a house on Merritt Street just off Gulf Beach Highway. He had two biological brothers (Terrance and Terrell), but his mother, Katrina Richardson, welcomed many in her home throughout his life. She raised 11 children as a foster parent. She worked three jobs, including at seafood restaurants, daycare centers, and as a maid. He was raised by his mother and grand-mother, who drove the city bus for 40 years. Richardson didn't know his biological father. The only thing he ever knew was his father had at least 11 children and passed away. His mother was a positive influence when it came to hard work and providing for family. The living situation just may not have been ideal. "Warrington is the craziest, most beautiful place in the world to me," Trent said. "It was amazing to grow up there. We went through the good and the bad. It's amazing to overcome everything. Being broke was rich to us. When it came supper time, it was every man for himself."

It was a neighborhood full of nightly gunshots and drug deals. That was the life Richardson knew. He does not regret where he was raised. He believes those influences could have taken him down a different path, but the ones who were working the streets saw something in him. They did not want Richardson to follow in their path. They did not want his future as another hustler on the street. "Those were the guys who raised me," he said. "There were a lot of drug deals going down. They weren't necessarily a role model to me, but they were positive of my life because they would tell me this isn't my life. They would tell me to stay off these streets."

His older brothers played football, and both were defensive players. Richardson's mother allowed him to start playing football when he was 6 years old. It was an escape from the daily life in Warrington. Richardson has always played on the offensive side of the ball. However, he began his career as an offensive lineman. The early days were spent playing sandlot football at Myrtle Grove Park and basketball at the Salvation Army. Richardson made the transition to running back during his third year playing for the Myrtle Grove Eagles and never looked back. He led his team to four straight peewee championships. The biggest rival, the Salvation Army, had two future NFL stars in running back Alfred Morris and wide receiver Doug Baldwin. "Talent-wise they should have been blowing teams out," Richardson said. "Morris actually played on the offensive line until the fourth grade because they were so good. Doug Baldwin was always the guy you didn't want to play against. Everyone knew who Doug was. He was the guy. They were a year older, but they never beat us. We would always beat them in the championship. They were more talented, but we were more organized. We were going to block to death, hit you, and gang tackle. We were going to make sure the job was done."

Richardson started learning there was life outside of Warrington Village. He was told the life he was accustomed to was not all that was available. His Little League coach, Tom Williamson, would let him stay at his house on the weekends to show a different side of the world even if it was only a few miles away. He learned the way of the gun was not for him. He stayed away from the negative influences, and football and other sports were giving him an opportunity to have a better life. He remembers how "stupid" it was for friends to fight each other for no reason other than because they were living in a different community.

Terrance and Terrell were five years and two years older, respectively. Both had also played on the same fields at Myrtle Grove, which was a few miles away from Escambia High School. Both were successful football players during their high school days. Terrell signed with Louisiana-Lafayette in 2007. Trent had a close relationship with his middle brother as the two were the only ones who also had the same father. All the children his mother adopted played football. From sandlots to PlayStation 2, it was a competitive household.

Trent suffered back-to-back injuries during the freshman and sophomore year at Escambia High School. It was the same play call and same injury. Escambia ran a Wing-T offense with head coach Ronnie Gilliland. In the third game of the season against Rutherford High School in Panama City, Florida, Richardson took a pitch on the left side from the quarterback. He was taken out beneath his legs and tore two ligaments in his left ankle. He finished the game as a decoy, but his season came to an end after screws were inserted.

That was not the only twist during his high school career. Richardson will not forget the moment his mother approached him during his freshman year and turned his world upside down. "My mom came to me and asked, 'What was we going to do about this baby?'" He said. "My older brother, Terrell, was having a baby. I told my mom we were going to help take care of Terrell's baby. She said, 'No, what are we doing about your baby?' I said, 'What baby?' I didn't know what she was talking about. She found out from the girl's mom. She knew before I did."

Sevina Fatu gave birth to Taliyah, Richardson's first daughter when he was a sophomore in high school. The couple would have another daughter, Elevera, two years later.

Richardson returned from injury ready for a breakout sophomore campaign. There was a lot of build-up for the second game of the season against Washington High School in Pensacola. But then the same injury occurred on the same play but to a different ankle. "I'm thinking, *This sport just isn't for me*," Richardson said. "I had just had my first child. I was told I wouldn't be able to run really well again. My whole self-esteem about football and sports was shot. I knew it was over."

Richardson decided to suck it up, rehab his ankle, and keep fighting for respect and redemption on the gridiron. He was not just fighting to get out of the streets of his neighborhood. He did not want his daughter to grow up with the same things he experienced. He was a sophomore, coming off two season-ending injuries, and was raising a daughter. He could have resorted to the street life in order to provide, but it was the time he spent working at a breakfast and lunch buffet in Orange Beach, Alabama, that re-focused his attention. "I worked with prisoners, who were in a work-release program," he said. "They challenged me every week. They kept me out of trouble. They were able to teach me about how they messed up and what they should have done differently. They said I have one chance at this and 'don't mess up the opportunity.' They'd give me a new challenge every week."

Richardson found a bluff filled with sand, which has now become known as "Trent Richardson Bluff." He ran up and down the sand hills of the bluff almost daily. It improved his speed and strength. He could not find anyone who would join him. It became Richardson's trainer, his escape, his home away from home. It was the sand hills that made the improvement he needed during the final two years of his high school football season. He developed quick twitch muscles and his explosive skills on that bluff. He had success in track during the spring of his sophomore year, and after the time on the sand hills, it was finally his time to shine.

Nichols became the head coach, and the offense switched to an I formation. The fire was ignited, and Richardson rushed for 407 yards in the opening game of his junior season against Tate High School. He played in eight games and rushed for 1,390 yards and 13 touchdowns. He got hit on his ankle late in the season, which sidelined him for the remaining two games, but it was not as serious as the previous two injuries. He was named second team All-State in Class 5A. "Nobody really knew much about me," Richardson said. "I had a good junior season, but we didn't make the playoffs. I never played in a playoff game my entire high school career. I didn't go up against much talent until I played in the Under Armour All-American Game after my senior season. People thought I was fragile. I had to really fight through people labeling me that. They didn't know my work ethic. They didn't know how hard I really ran. You could see on film I ran pretty hard. I was shifty and real fast. I was a football player who also ran track."

Former Alabama assistant coach Lance Thompson led the charge in recruiting Richardson for the Crimson Tide. Some may have worried about the ankle injuries. Alabama was not concerned. "Trent was an awesome kid," Thompson said. "He was just such a great talent. I wouldn't say we were ever nervous about the injuries. They were freak accidents. He was such a physically imposing and powerful young guy. He was a great teammate, and his spirit was just so uplifting. He then had the speed."

Alabama became the first school to extend Richardson a scholarship offer. He remembers when he spoke with Nick Saban and the impact of the conversation. Alabama had signed the No. 1 recruiting class in the country, according to Rivals.com, in 2008. Richardson started drawing comparisons to high school phenoms such as Herschel Walker and Bo Jackson because of his ability on the football field and in track. "Trent was big and he could run real fast," said former Alabama running backs coach Burton Burns, who is currently the running backs coach for the New York Giants. "The more we got to know him, watching tape and watching him play, we knew he was a guy who was a little different than what we had. He was different from Mark [Ingram]. He was a bigger, faster Mark is what we thought at the time. We thought based on the direction we were going to go offensively he would be a perfect fit. There was so much noise around him...Everyone was recruiting him. He was really a down-to-earth guy. It caught our attention. We wanted a guy who was going to be a team player."

On his first visit to Tuscaloosa, Richardson met Julio Jones, who became one of his closest friends during their time at Alabama. He remembers taking a visit to Auburn where his cousin, Tyrone Green, played and will not forget asking quarterback Kodi Burns for an autograph. Kodi Burns turned him away. That would add to the dislike between the two schools.

Having grown up in the Sunshine State, Richardson liked the big three: Florida State, Miami, and Florida. However, the University of Texas is where he always wanted to play. He loved running backs like the late Cedric Benson and Ricky Williams. He was also a big fan of Earl Campbell. And his favorite college football player growing up was former Texas quarterback Vince Young. One of his brothers came home from college one day. He placed pictures of a lot of great running backs on the wall: Williams, Barry Sanders, Benson, Smith, Jackson, and Walker.

Richardson took spring visits to various schools. He mesmerized people on the track and in weightlifting competitions. Many do not know how impressed he was with Mississippi State, who was coached at the time by former Alabama player and coach Sylvester Croom. The Bulldogs told him he could come in and start as a true freshman while Alabama was a running-back-by-committee offense with players like Glen Coffee, Terry Grant, Roy Upchurch, and Jimmy Johns. There was not a feature player. Ingram had yet to arrive. "One of the guys Trent really liked the most was Woody McCorvey," Boyd said.

Boyd was recruited in the mid-1980s by Coach McCorvey, who was a former Alabama assistant coach but recruited Boyd when he was at Clemson. Boyd ended up signing with the University of Virginia where he played wide receiver and kick returner from 1986 to 1989. Richardson was aware of the connection between Coach McCorvey, who was on the Mississippi State staff, and Boyd. He agreed to take a visit to Starkville, Mississippi. "I took Trent up there to meet those guys," Boyd said. "He met the staff and liked them. He saw the stadium and said, 'It's a small stadium.' Coach McCorvey said, 'Well, yeah, but you play in the SEC, so you will get to play in all the stadiums.'"

The spring visits ended on June 3, 2008. Richardson was on the phone with Coach Saban, who said he would love for him to go ahead and make a commitment. Saban told him could still enjoy his visits and have fun but was eager to go ahead and get him on the recruiting board. Richardson committed to Alabama, not really knowing how intense his recruitment would become. This was a 17-year old, who did not have his own bedroom until he arrived in college. He spent most of the time sleeping on the couch or on the floor. He now had powerhouse programs vigorously courting him to land his signature.

Urban Meyer had just completed his third season at Florida and remained in strong pursuit of Richardson. He was not aware a commitment to Alabama was in the cards. He often called Boyd. Many in the community were hoping Richardson would follow in the footsteps of Smith. Escambia High School's nickname was even the Gators. "The conversations I was having with Trent were more about where would he be comfortable if he were to get hurt," Boyd said. "You never know what's going to happen. Urban was not happy. He couldn't believe how I wouldn't know Trent was going to commit to Alabama. We just weren't having those conversations. People wanted him to follow the same page as Emmitt. He said he felt comfortable around the [Alabama] folks. I said, 'If that's where you are comfortable, then that's where you need to be.' He was 17 years old. He had between June and February to still take visits."

Richardson had a remarkable senior season with 2,100 yards rushing on 228 carries and 25 touchdowns, including that 419-yard performance in late September. Schools like Florida, Florida State, and LSU would not go away. There was plenty of belief in Gainesville that the Gators staff could flip Richardson away from the Crimson Tide. The Gators defeated Alabama in December in the SEC Championship Game (in Saban's second year in Tuscaloosa). Coach Meyer pulled out all the tricks to try and get Richardson on board. "I remember Urban came to visit me, and we went to King's Buffet," Richardson said. "He was around my kids and whole family. My kids' mom is Samoan. He starts speaking Polynesian to them. She didn't really speak, so she didn't know what to say. He would tell the kids to call him 'Uncle U.' He was kind of overdoing it. A Florida fan came up to me and asked me to sign an autograph for him before they asked Urban. He said it was the first time he had been with someone who got asked for an autograph before him. He kept trying to get me to decommit from Alabama. He asked me to secretly commit and he wouldn't tell anyone. His big selling point was Tebow was coming back. They had just won the national championship. He said they could have two 225-pound guys in the backfield. They were trying to sell me on running track with Chris Rainey and Jeff Demps."

Richardson took his first official visit to Alabama prior to his official visit to Florida. He had been to Tuscaloosa several times and had the same experience on most occasions. The visit to Florida was different the following week. He does not know what would have ultimately happened if he visited the Gators the final weekend before Signing Day. All the stops were pulled out to get him to flip. "My official visit to Florida was the most fun trip I went on," he said. "Joe

Haden was my official visit host. That trip was crazy. We went into every little bar. There was stuff set up for us. I remember going in one club with Joe Haden, who was like the mayor of Gainesville. He went up into the DJ booth and stopped the whole club. He was like, 'We have Trent Richardson in the house. Let's show him why he should be here.' They start playing the fight song, and everyone is doing the Gator chomp. They were chanting, 'Trent! Trent! Trent!' It was crazy. He said, 'This is the lifestyle if you come here.'

"My mom liked it down there, but she didn't like it more than Alabama. In the end I didn't go to Florida because they were so cocky. I mean, so cocky. They had just won the national championship. They were all talking about how they were going to win it all again the next year. Everyone was coming back: Tebow, Aaron Hernandez, Brandon Spikes, Will Hill, Ahmad Black, the Pouncey twins, Carlos Dunlap. They tried to sell me on being the starting guy in the backfield on what they thought was the best team ever. I could be with the best weightlifting crew and be on the fastest team in college football. Life was going to be good if I came there. They also tried to make Emmitt a big part of it. Alabama was just never cocky like Florida was. Florida was just so cocky on every trip I went on. I'm a recruit, and players on the team are in the dorm [are] showing me their high school highlight tapes. I know you were good in high school, you just won a national championship, but you want to show me your highlights from high school? It was stuff like that just turned me off from Florida."

Because Terrell was a defensive end at Louisiana-Lafayette, it helped LSU become a major factor in Richardson's recruitment. He knew the distance between the two schools would have been easier on his mom. He had a great time in Lafayette when he visited his brother. A strong relationship with former LSU running backs coach Larry Porter and an infatuation with a shrimp burger at a local restaurant almost won his heart. "My mom wanted me to go there so bad in the beginning," Richardson said. "She was coming home telling everyone I'm going to be a Tiger. For me there was nothing better than Alabama. Once she went on the trip to Alabama, she started saying, 'We are rolling with the Tide.' I also wanted to be different from my brother. I didn't want to be a distraction to him. I know he wouldn't have had a problem with it, but I didn't want to make it an issue. I just felt so comfortable with Bama. I didn't think LSU had anything more to offer than Alabama did. LSU was stacked at running back. Their big selling point was Alabama was running back by committee. It didn't really help them when they were playing four running backs, too. Coach Porter recruited me very hard. We talked all the time. He is one of the best recruiters out there in terms of bringing a guy in and making him feel comfortable. LSU had a good track program, too. I just loved the whole lifestyle. They have one of the best facilities around. I loved the education part. What stood out to me about it at the time was they had their own academic Players of the Week. Alabama wasn't doing that yet. They do now. I was also real competitive in education, too. They had a lot of positives going on."

Porter (currently the running backs coach at Auburn) enjoyed the relationship he built with Richardson during his time in Baton Rouge, Louisiana. He felt the Tigers had a good chance to flip him away from the Tide. "He was obviously one of our top recruits, and I took a lot pride in giving it our best shot," Coach Porter said. "We thought we had a real shot. He was making trips down I-10 to see his brother at Lafayette and would stop in to see us. I thought we had a great chance to land him, but in the end, we didn't. That's the beauty of what we do for a living. Sometimes you recruit guys [and] you build a relationship, which goes beyond recruiting. That's what Trent and I had. We built a real relationship. Even though he didn't come to LSU, we had enough respect for each other to sustain it, and I was one of his biggest fans. I wished him well throughout every game but one throughout the season. Some relationships you build way beyond the recruiting aspect, and certainly my relationship with Trent was one of those."

Richardson preaches to his children, "You are your way out." Things do not just happen. You have to make them happen. Richardson could have easily given up. He became one of the most sought-after recruits in the country. He built relationships with coaches, players, and other recruits. Alabama may have lost to Florida in the SEC Championship Game, but he connected with players like Jones, Ingram, Mark Barron, B.J. Scott, and Jerrell Harris. They were freshmen at Alabama who had the same mind-set. They were striving for greatness. They were not showing their five-star highlight film from high school. "Lance Thompson recruited me to Alabama and then he left for Tennessee," Richardson said. "Julio called me up and said, 'I hear you are going to decommit because Lance left.' I told him, 'I kind of felt betrayed because Lance left,' and Julio was like, 'He isn't even going to be your coach. You will hardly see him.' Julio then was like, 'If you want to go somewhere else, then go. We are still going to beat your ass.' I knew then I wanted to be on a team with guys who had the mind-set like that."

Dre Kirkpatrick, a consensus five-star recruit from Gadsden City High School in Alabama, became a close friend with Richardson during the process. The two took official visits together to Alabama

181

and Florida. Richardson knew Kirkpatrick would likely go to Alabama. He also became friends with Alabama signees like Nico Johnson, AJ McCarron, and D.J. Fluker. They were a tight-knit group. Richardson was still uncertain on Signing Day eve. He spoke with Smith, who gave him advice Richardson will never forget. "I asked him what would he do if he were me," Richardson said. "He told me for him to be greedy he would want me to go to Florida. He then said, 'With our running style, we needed to run out of the I formation. We needed to run downhill. Running out of the shotgun was a no-no for us.' He said he'd love for me to go to Florida because he went there. I'm a hometown boy. For him, once a Gator, always a Gator. He was like, 'If I was you making the decision right now, I'd go to Alabama.'"

On Signing Day on February 4, 2009, Alabama was closing with an incredible class. The morning started with commitments from Kirkpatrick, four-star lineman Brandon Moore, four-star linebacker Tana Patrick, four-star wide receiver Kenny Bell (who flipped from LSU), four-star wide receiver Kendall Kelly, and four-star running back Eddie Lacy. The No. 1 recruiting class for a second consecutive year was essentially a lock unless Richardson decided to flip his commitment to LSU. He eliminated the Tigers in his mind. He made a last-second phone call to Meyer. "I had been in a lot of communication with Urban," Richardson said. "I was signing at 4:00 PM. Right before I signed, I decided to call him one more time. I just wanted to hear what he had to say again and get a little more clarity. I had pretty much decided it was Alabama, but I just called him. If he would have answered the phone, I probably would have gone to Florida. He didn't pick up, and I just said, 'Forget it.' I wasn't even going to answer if he tried calling back."

Coach Burns knew things would get tight on Signing Day, especially after Lacy announced for Alabama that morning. Richardson knew about Alabama's pursuit of Lacy. Alabama wanted to get both. Even though Alabama didn't want to lose out on Richardson, they were not going to take a chance on missing out on both players. Richardson's announcement was attended by Alabama signees McCarron and Fluker. "[Richardson] told us he was going to sign with us," Burns said. "Guys say it all the time, and sometimes go elsewhere. The more you were around Trent, the more you felt like he was being honest. We told him to do it earlier that day, but he said the press conference was at 4:00 PM. That's what made us nervous. Coach Saban kept coming down to my office, asking what's going on with Trent. As nervous as we were, I felt like he was telling me the truth. It was crazy that day."

In the end Coach Saban and Coach Burns were monumental in securing Richardson's signature. The former five-star running back will never forget when Coach Saban had an in-home visit and heard gunshots going off in his neighborhood. Richardson knew Coach Saban had not been put in too many situations like that, but it was normal for the running back. It was just another day in his life. "When I came to Alabama and saw the tradition and the culture, I thought, *Why would I not want to get out of the situation I'm in,*" Richardson said. "*Why wouldn't I want to get out of Florida?* It was big for Coach Saban to be at my house that night and to be in that moment with me. He saw in my eyes I really wanted to get out of Pensacola. Coach Burns would always tell me the truth. I would have an opportunity to go to Alabama and do something good. Coach Saban…did promise me if I came there, worked hard, and did the right things, I would leave Alabama, become a first-round draft pick, and win a national championship. I won two national championships in three years at Alabama."

Tuscaloosa was Richardson's new home. The charismatic, always smiling, happy-go-lucky high school phenom made it out of the neighborhood. It was also Pensacola who made him. It was those sand hills in the bluff, his coworkers at the breakfast and lunch buffet, his high school coaches, Little League coach, his mom and grandmother, his brothers and his daughters who drove him to become the high school and college player he became. He played with Alabama greats. He said former Crimson Tide linebacker Rolando McClain was the best player he played with in Tuscaloosa, and Jones was the best overall athlete. He knew Alabama had the right ingredients to become a national championship contender.

Richardson joined forces with Ingram and Upchurch during his freshman season to become the nation's best backfield. Ingram won the Heisman Trophy. Alabama beat Florida in the SEC Championship Game and went on to win its first BCS National Championship in 2009. Richardson had 751 yards and eight touchdowns during the season, including 109 yards and two touchdowns in the Rose Bowl against Texas.

Richardson split carries the following season with Ingram. He finished with 719 yards and six touchdowns on the ground. He led the Crimson Tide to another BCS National Championship in 2011 with a win against LSU, which represented a rematch from the 9–6 loss to the Tigers earlier in the season. Richardson capped the year with 1,740 yards on the ground and 21 touchdowns. He finished third in the Heisman Trophy voting behind Robert Griffin III and Andrew Luck. He was a unanimous All-American, the Doak Walker

Award winner (given to the nation's best running back), and the SEC Offensive Player of the Year.

Richardson was drafted No. 3 overall by the Cleveland Browns in the 2012 NFL Draft. He had a successful rookie season with the Browns before getting traded in the middle of his second year to the Indianapolis Colts. He also spent time with the Oakland Raiders and Baltimore Ravens, but he struggled with injuries throughout his NFL career and finished with 1,469 yards and 14 touchdowns. Richardson currently resides in Trussville, Alabama, with his four children, Taliyah, Elevera, Trent Jr. (T.J.), and Ty'rell. "Trent is just a super kid," Thompson said. "People want to think about all the pro stuff, but he had an unbelievable career at Alabama. He was such a tremendous player. He was as good of a high school runner as there was, just a phenomenal talent...He really is a special cat."

Boyd remains a mentor and knows what drove Richardson as well as anyone. "He enjoyed the notoriety of being Trent Richardson," Boyd said. "I used to always tell Trent to go out the backdoor so he wasn't hounded by the media. He'd come out the front door without a shirt on. He wasn't trying to be cocky. He just loved making people feel good. He loved giving kids high-fives. Everyone was always pulling on him. He always tried to please everyone. He made the right decision. He and Coach Saban were the same guy. Trent likes to be treated special, but if you are honest with him, he can take it. I don't know anything that compares to Alabama football professionally or collegiately when it comes to the type of atmosphere it provides. People fight for their team. I know even when he was in the pros, he would get into it with anyone who talked about Alabama."

CHAPTER 16

T.J. Yeldon

The University of Alabama defeated LSU in the 2012 BCS National Championship. It was a rematch between the two teams after the Tigers defeated the Crimson Tide 9–6 in an overtime game dubbed the "Game of the Century" between the No. 1 and No. 2 teams in the country. Alabama won the rematch 21–0 against the Tigers on essentially LSU's home turf at the Superdome. Alabama blew out all opponents between September and November the following season, which included an opening destruction of No. 8 Michigan (41–14). LSU had suffered a tough 14–6 loss on the road to Florida. LSU won its next two games against No. 3 South Carolina and No. 20 Texas A&M to move back into the top five as Alabama traveled to Baton Rouge, Louisiana, on November 3. It was a revenge game for the Les Miles-coached Bayou Tigers.

The Crimson Tide went into Baton Rouge and built a 14–3 lead at halftime. Alabama looked atrocious to start the second half with back-to-back three-and-outs. The Tigers scored a touchdown to close the gap 14–10. Alabama had a pair of battering rams at running back in Eddie Lacy and true freshman T.J. Yeldon. But the freshman lost a fumble late in the third quarter inside the LSU 10-yard line. A score would have given Alabama a seven or 11-point lead. "AJ [McCarron] and I had missed a handoff, and LSU was able to go down and score," Yeldon said. "AJ came up to me after the play and said, 'Don't worry about it. We are going to need you. You are going to have to make a play in this game.' Ryan [Anderson] also came up to me and told me I was going to make a big play. Everyone was telling me that."

LSU milked the clock late in the fourth quarter. Alabama had not been able to move the ball at all the entire second half. The Tigers lined up for a 38-yard field goal, which kicker Drew Alleman missed. The momentum shifted. Energy on the Alabama sidelines had been restored. Confidence in the Alabama huddle led by McCarron was reignited. McCarron had gone 1-of-7 passing in the second half. He fired three straight completions to wide receiver Kevin Norwood. It was second and 10 on the LSU 28-yard line with one minute remaining in the game and Alabama trailing 17–14. Eli Gold, voice of the University of Alabama radio network, called the winning touchdown:

"AJ gets the snap. Pressure. Screen. Yeldon. 30, 25, 20. He's gonna go! He's gonna go! He's gonna go! Touchdown! T.J. Yeldon! T.J. Yeldon! On a screen, 28 yards. No flags. Alabama in what could be one of the epic comebacks in the Crimson Tide history takes a 20–17 lead with the extra point to come. Fifty-one seconds remaining in the ballgame."

Yeldon said it's still his favorite play. "I knew they were blitzing the guys off the edge," he said. "They did it on the previous two plays. I knew once I saw the play call if they were going to blitz again, it was going to be a big play. That was definitely one of the greatest plays of my college career."

That play left a stunned crowd in Death Valley on a Saturday night. LSU received the ball and returned it to the 20-yard line with 45 seconds remaining in the game, but there were no timeouts for the Tigers as they trailed 21–17. Alabama defensive lineman Damion Square sacked LSU quarterback Zach Mettenberger on third and 5 from the Tigers' 25-yard line to end the game and secure the SEC West for Alabama.

Approximately 11 months prior to the big game, Yeldon was a senior at Daphne High School in Alabama. He was graduating and set for early enrollment. He committed to Auburn prior to the start of his junior season. He made another decision on December 12, 2011, that would forever change his life. It was one of the biggest recruiting flips during the Nick Saban era at Alabama. The longtime Auburn commitment continued to say he was solid with the Tigers, but he released a statement the day before the recruiting dead period: "Over the last few weeks, I've really put a lot of time and thought into where I want to go to school and continue my football career. I am blessed to be in a situation where I have several great opportunities and I appreciate everyone involved who has helped me get to this point. I want to make an announcement so I can put this behind me and get to work on the things I need to do to prepare for college both athletically and academically. I am going to enroll at the University of Alabama in January. I have a lot of respect for Auburn, the coaches, and all of the people there, but at the end of the day, I feel like the University of Alabama is the best situation and fit for me and my family. I am 100 percent confident with my final decision. I feel great about it and I'm excited to get started."

Yeldon was born October 2, 1993, in Daphne, Alabama, to Tim and Kim Yeldon. He has an older brother, Brandon, and an older sister, Tianekka. He grew up playing various sports, including basketball and baseball. It was his grandmother, who passed away in 2005, who signed him up for youth football. Yeldon spent a lot of time playing sports at the Boys & Girls Clubs with friends like Anderson and Torren McGaster (a future three-year starter at cornerback for Vanderbilt).

Yeldon and Anderson were inseparable growing up as nearby neighbors and always at one another's house. Yeldon started playing football in sixth grade when he was part of the city league program. He was a quarterback in those days before eventually moving to running back once he arrived in middle school. "I liked the switch," he said. "I grew up watching guys like LaDainian Tomlinson and Reggie Bush. I wanted to play running back. Running backs were a big deal when I was growing up. I was only playing quarterback because I was the most athletic guy on the field."

Yeldon's time on the freshman team at Daphne was short-lived. He was talented enough to get called up but was often used in backup roles whether it was at slot receiver or running back. His father encouraged him to remain on the team despite wanting to play with his friends and start on the freshman team. He wasn't sure the point in just playing in mop-up duty when the Trojans would have a substantial lead in the game. "T.J. is one of those guys, who was really good in youth football and also really good in high school. Sometimes that doesn't always happen," said former Daphne head coach Glenn Vickery. "You could see early on T.J. was going to be a special player. When he was in middle school, nobody could tackle him once he touched the ball. You really could just tell early on he had a lot of ability as a running back and just an overall football player. We brought him up early during his freshman year. He was a big kid. He was a good slot blocker for us. I remember we played Pine Forest [in Pensacola, Florida] late in the season. They were a good team, but we had the game won. They kicked off to him, and he returned it for a touchdown."

The Trojans finished the 2008 season with a 7–3 record before losing to Theodore High School 7–6 in the first round of the state playoffs. Daphne was 5–6, which included a 35–7 loss to Fairhope (the first loss to them in 19 years) the following season, but did sneak into the state playoffs. The Trojans faced a rematch withTheodore, and Theodore was 9–1, heavily favored, and led by senior linebacker C.J. Mosley, who became a two-time All-American with the Crimson Tide, a Butkus Award winner, and first-round NFL draft pick.

Yeldon put on a show with 148 yards on the ground and two touchdowns for the stunning 41–19 upset win. Daphne then upset undefeated Fairhope 16–14 in the second round before falling to Auburn High School. The Tigers may have defeated Daphne, but Auburn running backs coach Curtis Luper was in attendance supporting his son, who was playing against Yeldon that night. "I saw him as a sophomore," Coach Luper said. "He was almost 6'2", 200 pounds. I knew he was a stud, no question about it. I made sure he knew after the game he had an offer from us. He came to camp the next summer and ran a 4.3. It solidified it for all of us. We definitely saw him as a running back. There are definitely some running backs that are special who are 6'2" or taller and can still play with pad level and still play behind their pads. He was one of those guys. He was able to get his pads down. Ultimately, he became a great college football player."

Yeldon received his second scholarship offer from Florida State before the floodgates really started to open, and offers poured in from top programs across the country. Alabama was a little late to the party. He was on Alabama's radar, but the staff was not going full throttle in recruiting him just yet. Alabama's early mistake may have been when Yeldon attended Junior Day in Tuscaloosa after his sophomore season. "We recruited T.J. for a long time," said former Alabama defensive coordinator and current Tennessee head coach Jeremy Pruitt. "Coach Saban told T.J. he reminded him of Mark Barron. Mark had played a little bit of offense in high school. T.J. was a really good athlete. He could play more than one spot. It wasn't long after that when T.J. committed to Auburn."

Auburn was all in from the moment it offered him. When then-Auburn offensive coordinator Gus Malzahn attended Yeldon's spring game, another visit to Auburn sealed the early commitment for the rising star. "My father and I were going up there so much," Yeldon said. "Coach Luper and I developed a good relationship. I felt like it was the right place for me at that time."

Daphne returned almost all of its starters from the 2009 season for Yeldon's junior year in 2010. The little bit of magic it found in the state playoffs the previous year returned. It was a perfect 15–0 season capped by a 7–6 win against Hoover High School in the Class 6A title game at Auburn's Jordan-Hare Stadium. Yeldon scored the game-winning touchdown on a one-yard run in the fourth quarter, ending Hoover's 21-game winning streak. Yeldon finished his junior season with 1,112 yards on the ground with 18 touchdowns. He also had 34 receptions for 504 yards and five touchdowns. "There is nothing better than winning a championship with the guys you grew up with," Yeldon said. "My sophomore year we basically had the same team. We just had not put it all together yet. Winning the state championship for your hometown and to do it with everyone you grew up with is one of the best moments of my life."

Yeldon is very quiet and reserved. He did not conduct many interviews throughout his high school days. Those close to him would say, "He may have been quiet, but he was always listening."

Yeldon must have been listening to Alabama, along with his best friend, Anderson (who committed to Alabama) because there were plenty of rumors of a possible flip from Auburn to Alabama. Those rumors were usually put to rest by Yeldon despite a few trips to the Capstone prior to his senior season.

Auburn won the National Championship in 2010, and Cam Newton captured the Heisman Trophy. It didn't come without controversy as the NCAA was looking into Newton's recruitment by the Tigers. "There was some stuff that happened," Yeldon said. "I thought they were going to take some punishment. I also had my guy, Ryan, in my ear all the time wanting me to come with him to Alabama. It was an everyday thing with him. Wallace Gilberry, who also had played at Alabama, is Ryan's cousin. He was always coming back to see us even when he was at Alabama. Every day Ryan was just like, 'Man, we can do this together, we grew up together, we went to Daphne, we can go to Alabama, and hopefully one day be on the same team in the league.' Alabama was also producing more NFL players than Auburn. He was always saying Auburn was going to get in trouble because of Cam. I mean, it was literally every day."

Former Daphne offensive coordinator Mike Vickery witnessed Alabama take a different recruiting approach to Yeldon between his junior and senior season. Yeldon went from a talented athlete, who could play multiple positions, to a bona fide high school All-American at the running back position. "Alabama had some questions," Mike Vickery said. "They knew T.J. was a good athlete, and he was a recruitable guy. They just weren't sure if he was a running back. That was probably a big sticking point. It all changed his senior year. His growth as a running back between his junior and senior year is as significant of a jump as I've ever seen. He was always a super athlete, super strong, but from a pure running back standpoint, his growth was off the charts. It was very obvious what that jump was and it became clear to Alabama."

Alabama moved forward and amped up its recruiting efforts. Pruitt had built a strong, close relationship with Yeldon and his family. Burton Burns and Saban were also forming a strong bond with him. He was no longer the player, who was a potential option for Alabama. Yeldon became a priority target and one the staff was willing to spend a lot of time recruiting to see if it had a chance to flip him from Auburn. "T.J. was an ultimate competitor," Coach Pruitt said. "He had great toughness. You watch him play. He had great vision. He was a slasher. He had great balance. He was just such a great competitor and athlete. There were a lot of positives."

Alabama signed future Heisman Trophy winner Mark Ingram in 2008. The Tide added Trent Richardson and Lacy in 2009. Who was going to become the next superstar in the backfield for Alabama? Burns (now the running backs coach for the New York Giants) had success developing running backs in Tuscaloosa. He thought Yeldon could be just as successful. "I only evaluated him as a running back," Coach Burns said. "He was different. His style was different from what we had. He was a little more upright in his running style. Guys like Mark and Trent were built from the ground up. T.J. was longer. We thought that was a unique talent with him. Other guys ran close to the ground. He worked higher. He had really good hands and quickness. He was hard to tackle. He never went down on the first hit. He was pretty sneaky in being able to make people miss in the hole."

Thoughts were creeping into Yeldon's head early in his senior season. He knew Alabama was the only other option as his parents wanted him to stay in state. "It was really at the beginning of my senior year when I started to really consider flipping to Alabama," Yeldon said. "I had become comfortable with the coaches there. I had built a good relationship with Coach Burns and coach Jeremy Pruitt. Coach Pruitt was always calling and talking to us. He was heavily recruiting me. I started taking more visits to Alabama with Ryan and got very comfortable up there. I also really liked Coach Saban. He had been in the NFL, and that was my dream. He had the resume of getting players to the NFL. He never sugarcoated anything. He was always straight up and honest. That's what sold us."

Auburn suffered significant losses on its team after the 2010 championship season, including Newton. The Tigers returned only four starters on offense and four on defense, which resulted in an 8–5 season and featured blowout losses to Alabama, Clemson, LSU, Arkansas, and Georgia. Malzahn was also heavily rumored throughout the season to leave for a head coaching position. He became the Arkansas State head coach in December. "The recruiting process was crazy," Yeldon's father said. "We told [T.J.] it was up to him. When he switched from Auburn to Alabama, it was his choice. We were behind him 100 percent. He wanted to make the switch. I remember Coach Malzahn saying how he wanted to build the offense around T.J. He then took the Arkansas State job. It was something that played a part in the decision. It's not about the coaches, but as a young kid, you see the offensive coordinator leave, it becomes a little bit of a factor."

Yeldon had a remarkable senior season with 2,193 yards on 232 carries and accounted for 31 touchdowns. He helped his team to a 9–1 regular-season record before it fell to Prattville High School in the second round of the playoffs. His playing days at Daphne had come to an end. Yeldon took an official visit to Alabama in early December prior to playing in the Alabama/Mississippi All-Star Game. It was during the visit in Tuscaloosa when he had changed his mind on his college choice. "I made the decision on my official visit to Alabama," Yeldon said. "Ryan and I were riding with Coach Pruitt around campus that Sunday. It was just the three of us in the car. That's when I told him I was going to make the switch. I sat down with my family and felt like it was the right decision for me. I was graduating high school early and knew there was a dead period coming up. Coach Pruitt told me schools couldn't talk to me once the dead period started. So that's when I made the switch right before the dead period, so no coaches could talk to me."

Alabama lost to LSU at home in 2011, and LSU went to the SEC Championship Game in December instead of Alabama. That loss had a silver lining. "We lost to LSU and didn't play in the SEC championship," Coach Pruitt said. "T.J. was supposed to come for an official visit early in the season with Ryan. A family member was sick or something like that happened. I don't think he could have taken an official visit with us if we didn't lose to LSU because there wouldn't have been a window for him to come visit. The week after the SEC championship, he played in the Alabama/Mississippi All-Star Game and then committed the next week."

The plan was set in motion. He was flipping to Alabama. Yeldon knew, his parents knew, Anderson knew, and a few of the Alabama coaches knew. The Vickerys, however, were not aware of a flip. There were other recruits at Daphne who were making decisions, taking visits, and entertaining college coaches throughout the recruiting contact period in December.

Yeldon and Anderson returned from their official visit weekend at Alabama and headed to Montgomery the following day for the Alabama/Mississippi All-Star Game. Luper was also at Daphne High School the following day to visit with Yeldon after his official visit with Alabama. "T.J. had accepted an award that morning from a local newscaster, Randy Patrick," Mike Vickery said. "As we were leaving the gym, I saw Coach Luper. I really didn't think anything about Alabama at that time. It didn't cross my mind there was any issue, but I could tell Coach Luper looked concerned. I went down to the fieldhouse. Ryan and T.J. had their luggage down there, packed, and ready to go to Montgomery. Luper was with T.J. I saw T.J. get on the phone and just asked after who it was. He said, 'Cam Newton.' I thought that's pretty cool. I didn't ask anything else about it. We left for Montgomery."

Yeldon was around other Alabama commitments throughout the week, which included Anderson, Reggie Ragland, and Alphonse Taylor (who flipped later from Florida State to Alabama). The team also had the No. 1 player in the state, Jameis Winston. Yeldon's head coach, Glenn Vickery, who worked as an assistant coach that week, loved the time he spent with the future No. 1 draft pick. He remembers most of the Alabama commitments were trying to get Winston to change his mind from Florida State and reconsider Alabama instead. Yeldon was seen as a solid commitment to the Tigers, though unbeknownst to others, he was on the cusp of making a stunning announcement. He even told reporters in Montgomery throughout the week that his commitment to Auburn was solid. "I was around the kids all week," Vickery said. "I rode up to Montgomery with Ryan and T.J. T.J. never mentioned anything to me about Alabama or indicated he was considering a flip. I remember during the bus rides I'd be sitting with Jameis. All the Alabama guys kept trying to get Jameis to flip. They were talking to him the whole time. T.J. hadn't mumbled a word about anything other than Auburn."

Yeldon was named the MVP of the Alabama/Mississippi All-Star Classic after rushing for 116 yards and three touchdowns in a 31–12 victory. He traveled back home to Daphne. His father then made a call to his high school coach the following Sunday. "Tim called and asked if they could meet with me at the fieldhouse," Glenn Vickery said. "So we meet at the fieldhouse. T.J. and his parents are sitting across the table from me. His dad said, 'Coach Vick, T.J wants to decommit from Auburn and commit to Alabama.'"

Glenn Vickery asked for confirmation from T.J. to make sure that is what he wanted to do. A firestorm from Auburn coaches, along with the media and fans, was about to take place. Vickery called Coach Luper to inform him and to speak with Coach Chizik. It was a phone call Coach Luper had expected for a while. "We got word that it was potentially going to happen around October or November," Luper said. "We kind of knew it was inevitable. When Coach Vickery called me on that Sunday, I told him when I answered I knew that call was coming. We had been told about a month earlier he was going to make the switch, and it was going to happen the day before the dead period. I told Coach Vickery [that] I knew he was going to call today."

Coach Luper had spent three years recruiting Yeldon and was disappointed in losing the high-caliber prospect but also held no ill will towards Yeldon. "It's the nature of the business," he said. "It's a necessary evil. You win some, you lose some. T.J. is a great young man. Every time we played against them, I got a chance to see him after the game and shake his hand. I would always tell him he was doing a great job and I was proud of him. I still follow his career."

Yeldon was not much of a talker. He let his high school coach speak on his behalf that Sunday of his flip to the University of Alabama. It was a tough decision. He had a relationship with Auburn from when Coach Luper first saw him play against Auburn High School during his sophomore season. "I never told them," Yeldon said. "I flipped the day before the dead period. That was the plan. Coach Pruitt set it up for me. I got a lot of hate mail and hate from people in my city because of it, people who didn't want me to go to Alabama. I dealt with it. At the end of the day, it was my decision. My parents were going to support me wherever I decided to go. I felt like Alabama was the right fit for me. Coach Vickery was always supporting me. He would always tell me to make sure I am comfortable going there. They were always going to support me no matter what. They wanted me to respect everyone and do it the right way. They always wanted me to work hard."

Coach Pruitt helped orchestrate the flip as much as he could on his end. He knew Yeldon would take a lot of heat for flipping from one in-state SEC program to the other. The best solution was to wait until the day before the dead period, which is prior to the early signing period. Recruits just had to enroll in January rather than sign in December, but that move could help keep the wrath off him a bit. He did not conduct any interviews and would not have any coaches visit his school or any further contact.

Yeldon's flip was a monumental decision, especially from a perception standpoint at the time. A year removed from winning a national championship, Auburn had finished 8–5, lost its offensive coordinator, and lost its prize in-state recruit to Alabama. The Vickerys took the brunt of Yeldon's decision. Fans accused them of pushing him to Alabama, which was not the case. Some fans even caused minor damage to one of their homes. "T.J. announced the decision on Sunday. My house was egged on Monday," Glenn Vickery said. "People were upset. People were asking how much did Mike Vickery get paid? I never got in the way of any of our kid's decisions. If a kid wanted to go to Notre Dame, that's their call. I selfishly wanted all my kids to stay in state and go to Alabama or Auburn so I could see them play more, but with social media now, you can keep up with the kids more than you could back then. To me it was a complete family decision. I loved Gene Chizik. I think he is a wonderful man. I think the world of him and Coach Luper. I know Mike took some heat, but we did it the right way. Some blamed us for not doing it the right way. Some thought we just released the statement, but before we did anything, we contacted Auburn and talked to [Luper,] who had been there with T.J. for three years, and talked to Coach Chizik before we released the news."

The No. 2 ranked running back in the country liked the family environment at Auburn. It is what made him fall in love with the program from the start of his recruitment. There were many things that played in favor for Alabama in the final year before he enrolled at the Capstone, which included the Newton allegations and Malzahn potentially leaving Auburn. In the end Alabama won him over for everything it had to offer. Ingram had won a Heisman Trophy at Alabama in 2009. Richardson had just won the Doak Walker Award (given to the nation's top running back). He could play with his best friend, Anderson, in college and also be coached by Burns and Saban. "I loved Auburn," Yeldon said. "It was a family thing. They would always say you are going to be family forever, but then I was going to Alabama and spending time with Coach Burns. He laid it straight out for me. He would say you have to do this and do that to be able to play. That was the main thing. I didn't want anyone sugarcoating it. I just want you to be straightforward and [hear] what it's going to be like when I get there. The recruiting process is all about trying to get you there, get you there, get you there. Coach Burns was saying, 'Everyone is going to make you feel good about coming there. I'm going to tell you how it is. If you work hard, you learn what you need to do, you are going to have a chance to play on the field.' I feel like I would have still flipped to Alabama even if there wasn't any talk about Auburn getting in trouble with the NCAA. Coach Malzahn left for Arkansas State. I had also developed a great relationship with Burton Burns, which really sold me."

Coach Burns knew Alabama was in strong contention for Yeldon's signature. The man who developed every Alabama running back between 2007 and 2017, which included Derrick Henry, Ingram, Richardson, Lacy, and Kenyan Drake, has heard recruits say they are going to flip or commit to Alabama. But you never know if it's just a rumor until it actually happens. "T.J. was really quiet," Burns said. "I talked to his mom and dad to get a better sense of how things were going. I wouldn't want to play poker with T.J. That's just what made T.J., T.J. You just weren't really sure what he was going to do. We knew there was something that attracted him to us. You couldn't quite put your finger on it. Maybe it was his presence. He seemed really interested. I honestly couldn't tell one way or the other what was going to happen. I didn't feel like we were chasing him. I thought it was 50/50 all the way. He never said too much, but he's a real good listener. He was always paying attention. He knew what was going on."

Many Auburn fans may not have understood at the time why Yeldon flipped. He was committed for such a long time and was the face of the Tigers recruiting class. Some fans thought the Daphne coaching staff had an agenda. Mike Vickery, who also served as the recruiting coordinator, handled more than Yeldon's recruitment. McGaster and Eric Lee (South Florida) were also going through the final days of their journey. Other players on the team were also recruited. "We had so many guys that year," Mike Vickery said. "With T.J. you saw some things coming with Auburn with some of the coaching turnover at Auburn. Alabama kind of had a perfect storm of guys who were leaving. They had another back [Drake] in their class and only planned on signing two backs that year. There was a spot at Alabama to play early. You kind of saw it turning for him during the middle the year.

"For us as coaches, it was never about colleges. It was always about the kids. We were going to support them no matter what and give our best advice. It may have made some fans upset, but we try to educate everyone on how to handle things. Kids have to make the best decision for themselves and for their future. We try to protect them any way we can. I wanted to limit as much negativity as I could from him. I wanted to take the heat off of him. The in-state stuff is a different animal, especially with those two schools and the fanbases. There was speculation on things that happened that went along with the decision, but it calmed down pretty quick. It all happened so fast. He flipped, then the dead period hit, he graduated, went to the U.S. Army All-American Game, and then enrolled at Alabama. It was all over."

The father-son coaching duo of Glenn Vickery and Mike Vickery were a big part of Yeldon's recruitment. They were not influencers on his decision but always had his back. Yeldon trusted them. "Those will always be my guys," Yeldon said. "They taught me a lot of things. I loved spending time with them. I loved being around Coach Vick and his kids. It's always something I will cherish. They were my first real coaches. They took me in. I really had the best time with those guys. They always supported me."

Yeldon was named Mr. Football in the state of Alabama after his senior season. He was also named Super All-State and Class 6A All-State. He was a five-star recruit and ranked the No. 2 running back in the country in 2012, according to Rivals.com. Yeldon enrolled early at Alabama. He was part of a recruiting class, which featured his best friend, Anderson, along with stars like Amari Cooper, Landon Collins, Drake, Ragland, Cyrus Jones, and Dalvin Tomlinson.

Yeldon played in every game as a true freshman at Alabama, rushing for 1,108 yards and 12 touchdowns. He had 153 yards rushing in the SEC Championship Game against Georgia and rushed for 110 yards and a touchdown in a win against Notre Dame in the 2013 BCS National Championship. He rushed for 1,235 yards and 14 touchdowns during his sophomore season. Alabama lost to Auburn in the infamous Kick Six game to end the Tide's quest to three-peat as national champions and then fell to Oklahoma in the Sugar Bowl.

Yeldon split carries with future Heisman Trophy winner Henry during his junior season and recorded 979 yards and 11 touchdowns. Alabama finished the season 12–2. The Tide lost early in the year to Ole Miss and to Ohio State in the college football playoff semifinals. Yeldon finished his career with a 2–1 record against Auburn, won two SEC Championships, and one BCS National Championship. He was a first team All-SEC selection in 2013 and second team All-SEC in 2014. Yeldon decided to forego his senior season and entered the 2015 NFL Draft. He was picked in the second round, the same round Anderson would be selected in two years later, by the Jacksonville

Jaguars. "I made it to the NFL," Yeldon said. "That was the goal. If I could do it again, I would always make the switch. Going to Alabama was one of the best things that ever happened to me, just meeting different people and having that brotherhood. I met some of my closest friends to this day at Alabama. The relationships I still have with the people at Alabama—coaches, trainers, everyone who is there—is why I feel I made the best decision. They always supported and took care of me. I wouldn't change it for nothing."

His parents were proud of the way he conducted himself throughout his football career. They were happy about his decision to flip to Alabama. They trusted the process and Saban. Yeldon won a championship in Little League, in high school, in college, and hopefully one day in the NFL. "He has always been a humble kid," his father said. "We did our best. He stayed out of trouble. I'll never forget Nick Saban coming down here and visiting with us. He told us the truth. He told us everything he expected, and everything he told us came true. I never got any hard feelings from people about T.J.'s flip. You have your Alabama and Auburn friends. If they don't want to be my friend because my child flipped, then we weren't friends to begin with. It was T.J.'s decision. It was the best choice of his life. He made the right decision. We loved it."

CHAPTER 17

Rashaan Evans

Rashaan Evans was the No. 14 overall player in the country in the Rivals100 in the class of 2014. He attended Auburn High School in Auburn, Alabama. He was an Auburn University legacy and so a lock to play college football at Auburn, right? Plus, Auburn had just beaten Alabama in the Iron Bowl. It was a huge win in November for the Tigers. Evans was excited after the game. The local five-star player was not expected to send shockwaves through the recruiting world on Signing Day in February.

Instead his announcement was one reason the Rivals.com website temporarily crashed as fans were posting their shock-and-awe reactions. The Auburn University official athletic website put up a new signee profile of Evans a few minutes prior to his announcement because they were expecting the hometown Tigers to land his signature. The premature post indicated to Alabama fans and several coaches there was no reason to watch the ESPNU broadcast from Auburn High School. Minutes later, however, Evans announced: "I will be attending the University of Alabama." He said that with a big smile as he placed the Alabama cap on his head in front of his high school friends, family, teammates, and the national TV audience.

The story of Rashaan Evans really began in the early 1980s when his father, Alan Evans, was a star running back for Enterprise High School in Alabama. He rushed for more than 3,100 yards during his high school career, was named a *Parade* All-American, and was recruited by many schools, including Alabama and Auburn. Evans chose the Tigers and joined an Auburn class, which featured the 1985 Heisman Trophy winner Bo Jackson.

When Evans' career in Auburn didn't pan out like most expected, he ended his career at UT Chattanooga. He returned to the city of Auburn to marry Chenavis in 1986 and raise his family. This was an Auburn family through and through despite Alan not having an awe-inspiring career on the Plains. Rashaan's mother holds several degrees from Auburn, including a doctorate in industrial and organizational psychology. Alan took Chenavis on their first date to Country's Barbecue in Auburn after she finally gave in to providing her phone number after multiple attempts. "I remember asking [my Auburn teammate] Clayton Beauford who she was, and he told me to forget about it," Alan recalled. "I said 'that's the prettiest woman I've ever seen in my life.' She wouldn't give me the time of day at first, but I saw her a few months later and asked her again if I could take her out. She finally gave me her phone number, and it all started from there."

Alan and Chenavis later married and have five children (from oldest to youngest): Sireka, Rashaan, Alex, Alexis, and Ashley. Sireka was a cheerleader at Auburn.

Alan remembers Rashaan had the look of a future football star the moment he laid eyes on him in the hospital. "When Rashaan was born, I was in the emergency room with his mom," he said. "He was the first boy we had. I knew when he was born he would be an athlete. He was all muscle and big. I thought this is the one—the chosen one. It's like he was born to do what he is doing. I spent a lot of time with him at an early age, but a lot of the things he learned how to do in terms of football he learned on his own. We knew he was heading in the right direction. He just needed some encouragement. I started coaching football when he was in first or second grade. I had a great time. I always played him up against guys who were a year or two older. They would beat him up, but I knew that's what it was going to take in order for him to have the opportunity. He responded very well. He got banged up and beat up, but it got to a point where he could hold his own against the guys who were older."

Rashaan remembers his younger days when he was on the field with his father teaching him the game. "At an early age, football was everything to me," he said. "I slept with my helmet on. I slept with my pads on. That's just who I was. Football was introduced to me pretty much at birth by my father. My father played with Bo Jackson at Auburn. He had his own experience as a *Parade* All-American. He wanted to pass the torch down to me to play football and hopefully take it to the next level which was the NFL, and it's exactly what I did. I had aspirations of playing other sports, but football just came naturally to me. Football made the most sense."

Evans always played against older teammates and was also a quarterback. He considered the position his best and assumed that's where his future was the brightest. Former Auburn High School head coach Tim Carter knew Evans from an early age. "I remember Rashaan as a seventh grader," Coach Carter said. "Back in middle school, you played both ways. He was playing quarterback. He was extremely tall for his age back then and he had a good arm. He was always athletic. He went through seventh and eighth grade, and then we pulled him up to the varsity in the ninth grade. He hurt his leg during spring practice, which really set him back as far as playing quarterback. We also had Cam Luper [a TCU signee] at the time. The injury took him out of the race, but he came back from the injury. We decided to put him on defense because he would come up and hit you. He was really good on defense. Our defensive coordinator Anthony Jeter and I thought he could be such an impactful player on the defensive side of the football. We had an injury at defensive end during his sophomore year. We put him in at defensive end during the first round of the playoffs. He had two sacks in the game. From that day on, he was a no-brainer for us. He was a staple to our team."

Coach Carter had a feeling the move from the offensive to the defensive side of the ball may have caused some friction but may not have known Evans was strongly considering a transfer before talking to his mom. "I had to make that move to defense and I really didn't like it," Evans said. "I wanted to play quarterback. I expected to play quarterback. Coach Jeter basically told my Pops, 'We are going to move your son to defense. We feel like he can be a really good player for us on defense.' My Pops and I felt kind of ill about it. This is not what we had planned. We really thought I could do something at quarterback. We felt like at the time we needed to transfer. We thought about it plenty of times. We thought about going to Opelika, which was our rival. We thought about Smiths Station. We thought about all these different places where we could go play quarterback. One person who really helped change my mind was my mom. She is the type of person, who is really good at figuring things out. She was just saying to stay put and stay at home. I should just work my way up in order to get opportunities to earn scholarships and prolong my football career. That's what I did. I am glad I did it. It was a blessing for me to get recruited by so many different schools not only in the SEC, but the Pac-12, the Big Ten, Big 12, and all other different conferences."

Evans played several sports growing up, which included football, basketball, and track. By his sophomore year in high school, he knew what he wanted to do in life. Evans decided to shut down his participation in other sports while focusing solely on football. "They moved him to defense and one day during his sophomore year they moved him back to quarterback because Luper was hurt or something," his father said. "Rashaan ran an option play. It was just a fluke accident. He faked to the fullback and turned it up and ran. A young safety came up and hit him. He fell to the ground and couldn't get back up. I was at practice that day. Coach Carter told me it didn't look good. I took him to the hospital. They X-rayed it and said he had a crack in his shin. We thought at that point it might be it because we knew it was going to be a long process to get back."

Auburn High School received a big addition to its program in the spring of 2012. Five-star linebacker Reuben Foster transferred to Auburn from Troup County High School in LaGrange, Georgia. He was the consensus No. 1 linebacker in the country. He had committed to Alabama early in the process but was keeping his recruitment open. He was taking visits and flipped to Auburn before eventually signing with the University of Alabama. Foster, however, may have opened the first door for Evans. "My first offer was from Georgia," Evans said. "They came to see Reuben Foster play in our spring game before my junior season. Georgia saw me play, they fell in love with me, and offered me right on the spot. That's when things really started to fall in line. Once other schools saw Georgia had offered me, they all started offering me. The offer from Georgia was really a big moment in my life. It all happened really fast after that."

Coach Carter recalled that, too. "We were playing Stanhope Elmore in the spring before Rashaan's junior season," Carter said. "Coach [Kirk] Olivadotti from Georgia was there. We had a who's who of college coaches there that night to see Reuben. We knew Rashaan was a [Division] I player, but he was young, and we knew it was still kind of early for him. Coach Olivadotti came running up to me after the game was over. He said, 'Who is No. 4?' I said, 'That's Rashaan Evans.' He said, 'Well, he was the best player on the field that night.' I don't think it was a slap at Reuben at all. He was just so impressed with how well Rashaan played. They offered him immediately. Auburn offered pretty soon after and they had already been champing at the bit for him. Those two are really the ones who started it for Rashaan."

Alabama continued to evaluate exactly where he fit in with its system. He had an "offer" from the school but still needed an in-person camp evaluation in the summer prior to his senior season for Alabama to really take its recruitment to the next level, though the Tide had shown interest since his freshman year. "He was a hard evaluation for us at linebacker because he played defensive end in high school," said Tyler Siskey who served as Alabama's recruiting coordinator. "It was getting hard to find inside backers for a 3-4 because if they were the size and speed you wanted, they were playing defensive end in high school. We knew he was very talented but very hard to evaluate. We really wanted to see him in camp. I remember he showed up to camp. He was late getting there. I don't think he even stretched. He put on his cleats and ran a 40. I think I clocked him at a 4.58 just coming out of the car. He was one of the fastest times we had in camp that summer. Every kid thinks they ran a 4.4. That's not true. So when he ran that 4.58, it was very impressive."

Evans, though, almost didn't attend the camp. "It was our first week of summer workouts," Carter said. "Alabama was having its football camp. Alan called me up and said they were going to run down to Alabama for the day. Rashaan was going to work out for them. I told him Rashaan had a ton of big offers and I really didn't want him to get hurt. I remember Alan telling me that Rashaan did the camp and went up against the best offensive lineman in the country from Louisiana, Cam Robinson. He said Rashaan had a field day in pass rushing drills, and Coach Saban was trying to get him to commit. I mean it went from lukewarm interest from Alabama to he was at the top of their recruiting board. It's kind of a funny story because the first person to ever take him to Alabama was Karibi Dede, who played at Auburn. I believe Rashaan was a freshman at the time. I think that's when Rashaan really first found out about Alabama. He had been in Auburn his whole life. His parents went to school there. It's all he knew. That's when he really first fell in love with Alabama. Then he goes back and has the camp performance against Cam Robinson and just had a really good day overall down there. That's when he really went to another level with Alabama."

Evans knew it took Alabama a little longer than others to start heavily recruiting him but wasn't sure why. He had scholarship offers from several programs prior to the start of his junior season. "I just remember it was later in the season when they started showing more interest," Evans said. "I was playing really good, and more schools were coming to the games. What made things even better is having another five-star there in Reuben. It gave me a lot of publicity at that time. Colleges were wondering who I was. Reuben was still committed to Auburn during that time, but then Alabama was back in it with him, and he eventually flipped. I think Alabama knew once

Reuben signed and he had been there for a little bit that he could help sway me. To be honest, I wanted to play with him. We really became close. He is one of the most athletic players I have ever been around. Reuben checked all the boxes of what you look for in a football player. He was powerful, fast, really good instincts. He helped elevate your game. He was going 100 miles per hour downhill with no regard for his body. He made you want to play at a different level. He was the tone setter. He was just naturally gifted like a Ray Lewis type. Everyone respected him and knew what kind of athlete and player he was, just a naturally gifted athlete. That's what sums up Reuben Foster."

Evans saw his close friend become the player he envisioned at the college level: All-American, Butkus Award winner, national champion, first-round pick in the NFL. Injuries and off-the-field issues, though, hindered Foster's start to his career in the NFL. "He was the best player I played with during my time at Bama," Evans said. "I would rank him right at the top. He was just so naturally gifted. It's just crazy to think about his whole situation. People talk about how great Luke Kuechly and Bobby Wagner are in the NFL, but I guarantee if Reuben stayed healthy and on the right track, he would blow those guys out the window. He checked every box you look for in a linebacker. He had unlimited hitting power, unlimited instincts. He could run down any guy. His presence on the field was like Patrick Willis or Ray Lewis."

Although Auburn and Georgia may have assumed it had the upper hand in the early stages of his recruitment, Evans admits it was two other programs garnering his attention. "It was Tennessee and UCLA," he said. "That's who I really liked early on. Then I started falling back in love with Auburn. I spent a lot of time over there with the coaches and players. I went to several games. They were showing a lot of interest in me. Auburn really started swaying me during my senior season. I was thinking Auburn was going to be the one, but then I took my official visits. UCLA was definitely my favorite official visit. You go see palm trees and Hollywood. You meet other players out there. It really seduces you. There is a lot of promise out there. It's not just football. It's just a beautiful city. It was very attractive. I will definitely say UCLA was the best place I visited."

Evans had an incredible senior season with 54 tackles, 17 sacks, 12 tackles for loss, 20 quarterback hurries, five pass deflections, and three forced fumbles. He helped Auburn High School win a region championship and guided the team to its first appearance in the Super Six state championship. He was named the Class 6A Lineman of the Year, earned All-State honors, and was named the *Opelika-Auburn News* Defensive Player of the Year.

Evans participated in the Under Armour All-American Game, was named a five-star recruit by Rivals.com, won MVP in the Alabama/Mississippi All-Star Classic, and was named a first-team *Parade* All-American (just like his father). "He was clearly an exceptional player," said Rhett Lashlee, the former Auburn offensive coordinator and current offensive coordinator at the University of Miami. "Everyone knew his best days were ahead of him. He was long, athletic. He was a high priority for us."

The pressure started to mount late in the recruiting process. It's not something to take lightly, especially in an Auburn family. A decision other than Auburn was going to have a lasting impact. "We weighed all of that," Alan said. "We knew life as we knew it would never be the same again if Rashaan decided to go against the grain. I was an Auburn man. My wife was born and raised in Auburn.

She has five degrees from Auburn. She was on just about every major board at Auburn. My daughter was an Auburn cheerleader. We were constant guests at the president's house. My wife and Coach Dye are best friends. I would go to Coach Dye's ranch on the weekends. Coach Dye and his wife knew Rashaan before anybody. That's how deep it was. I knew it would be harsh if we decided to go somewhere else."

Lashlee was in charge of Evans' recruitment throughout the process. He was on a tag team with Rodney Garner, who had a prior relationship with Evans' father. Lashlee thought Auburn was in good shape, especially after the Iron Bowl. "I honestly still think Rashaan wanted to come to Auburn," Lashlee said. "He came to a ton of games as a recruit. He was there for the Kick Six Game. When we returned the kick six, I remember Kirby [Smart] and I were both on about the [opposite] 30-yard line closest to the end zone where we had just scored. We are both in shock for different reasons. We were going to meet each other to shake hands after the game, and Rashaan came running by me screaming in excitement, like can you believe this? He was genuinely fired up. This was basically around Thanksgiving, and you're thinking this kid wants to be here. It was such an epic moment it probably didn't matter. That was really the last memory I had before the birthday party."

That party was a hot topic on all football messages boards, especially on the Alabama and Auburn boards during the final weekend before Signing Day. "It was my grandfather's 80th birthday party," Evans said. "It was amazing. We told coaches from both sides that if they wanted to come to the birthday party, that's where I would be. I think both sides were thinking we are going to go, and this might help sway him. They didn't realize the other side was coming, too."

Auburn was represented by Gus Malzahn, Lashlee, Garner, Dameyune Craig, Scott Fountain, Melvin Smith, and Charlie Harbison. Alabama sent Smart, Bo Davis, Burton Burns, and Lance Thompson. "I was dancing with my mom and kept having to go back and forth to each side to visit with Auburn and Alabama. I really don't even remember seeing the coaches interact with each other. It was like an old western standoff. Kirby was really funny out there. He is one of those guys. When he is having a good time, he is fun to be around. He took the initiative to go out on the dance floor. He started dancing with my auntie. That in itself probably helped sway me toward Bama on that final weekend before Signing Day."

Coach Carter had seen his fair share of the top echelon of college coaches come through his program because he top players like Dee Finley, who played at Florida, and Foster. He was accustomed to top schools recruiting his best players. "Rashaan waited so long to commit," he said. "It got a little crazy. He was really laboring over his decision. He loved Alabama and Auburn. He also really loved UCLA. He really liked Los Angeles. I think Alan told him, 'You need to stay a little closer to home.' I think it bothered Rashaan to leave the Auburn community. I would always tell my kids to pick a school [that] if football ended tomorrow, you would be happy being a student there. Don't pick a school based on a coach. Of course, Coach Saban has more stability than any coach in college football. Rashaan's dad had been a *Parade* All-American in high school. He knew how to handle the process."

Evans gives a lot of credit to his parents who helped him reach his ultimate decision to go to Alabama. There were many reasons why he chose the Crimson Tide. Alabama checked every criteria he looked for in a school. He knew the decision was the hardest choice he would ever have to make at this point in his life, especially if he chose to leave the only town he ever knew to go to a school across the state and a bitter rival. "My mom was really the one who told me everything I really needed to look for when I took my official visits," he said. "My Pops did a really good job of keeping me level-headed. The college who really wants you is going to let it be known. It will be genuine. It's a feeling you will get, and when you know, you know. You will know which coach you really want to play for. I got that from Coach Saban.

"I will never forget walking into his office. It's as glamourous as you can make it. He is a rock star in college football. You walk into his office, and he has a button that closes the door. It's like 18' tall. It's already mind-boggling as a high school player just being in there. You come in there and sit down. He has all the rings laid out with lights flashing on them that makes it super bright. They are glaring at you. You can barely see him. He sits in his chair real comfortable and real confident. What makes him so unique is he is not sitting there lathering you up about how you're the best player, you're so good like all these other schools are constantly saying. I was hearing the same thing from every other school about how I was the best player and how I can change the program. Coach Saban doesn't do that. He is different from every other coach. He tells you what he can do for you. It's a bittersweet talk. You can be on the same stage with all these great athletes who have come to Bama and who are at Bama. You will have the chance to do all these different things, but then he hits you with: 'We aren't going to give it to you. You aren't going to be given a starting position. You will have to earn it. If you are the best, then you will play.' He hits you with that psychology. You really like hearing that as a high school recruit. I don't want to hear the same stuff about how great I am. I want to earn it. Coach Saban gets rid of the uncertainty though. He tells you what he wants you to be a part of and achieve. I visited all these other colleges: Auburn, UCLA. It just didn't give me the feeling statistics-wise. Which school was going to be the best for me? Which school was putting the best linebackers in the NFL at the time? Who was producing the most first rounders? We took all of that into account."

A main factor in his decision was really all about his future position. "What is best for him in the long run?" His father said. "We broke down the nuts and bolts of it all. The last [Auburn] linebacker taken in the NFL draft in the first round was Takeo Spikes [in 1998]. Auburn wasn't known for their linebackers. Auburn also wanted Rashaan to play the star position, which was more like safety. He had been playing with his hand in the dirt throughout his career. Ellis Johnson was the defensive coordinator at Auburn at the time. He had implemented the 4-2-5 defense, which has two linebackers and five defensive backs. We kept asking, 'What's Rashaan going to play at Auburn?' They said, 'Well, he will be more like a strong safety than a linebacker.' That's not really Rashaan. He likes to pass rush. They said he probably wouldn't be doing that. That didn't really sit well with Rashaan. We started to dig a little deeper on how they would use him.

"Coach Saban came and visited our house. He told Rashaan they would have him rush off the edge and give him an opportunity to play linebacker. They also said they thought his future was at inside linebacker. So we knew at some point if he went to Alabama, they would move him inside. We were fine with that. Coach Saban told him if he plays four years, there was a good chance he will be a first-round draft pick in the NFL. It came to fruition. It wasn't easy, but it happened just like Coach Saban said it would."

Still, the thought of going across the state to play for Alabama instead of the hometown team was a heavy burden to bear. Alan went through a similar recruitment. He didn't have the immense pressure of staying in his hometown, but he remembers how tough the decision was to commit to one in-state school instead of another. He continued to listen to what the coaching staff at Auburn had to say leading up to Rashaan's Signing Day ceremony. "Our recruitment was almost the same," he said. "I had the same pressures he had. I was very highly recruited. I was the No. 1 player at my position. I felt the same pressure, especially with it being between Alabama and Auburn. Most people in my town were split. When I made the decision to go to Auburn instead of Alabama, all of the Alabama people in my life fell out. The same thing happened to Rashaan. All the Auburn people fell out. I knew he was leaning toward Alabama after our last conversation with Coach Malzahn. Coach Malzahn actually had me come over to the football complex the night before Signing Day. He was trying to convince us that Auburn was the best school for Rashaan. We had become very close with Coach Malzahn and his wife. They really wanted Rashaan to come to Auburn. We tried our best to make it fit. It just didn't because of the way they wanted to play him. It didn't have anything to do with the school or the education. All it came down to was how they wanted to use him."

Alan and his wife informed Coach Saban of Rashaan's likely destination but also said he had the right to change his mind. The decision was completely up to him. He was torn because of his love for Auburn. "Signing Day really was the craziest moment of my life," Rashaan said. "The whole recruiting process was crazy because you go to all of these different colleges. They treat you all the same. Everyone loves you. Everyone wants you. Everyone tells you can help them win national championships. It makes you feel good. You eat it up. I have the opportunity to play at the biggest stage for an amazing college football organization like Alabama or Auburn or UCLA. They want you to be a part of their program, and it feels good. It becomes a bigger monster when you are trying to decide which school is the right one for you. A college helps morph you into the person you want to become, the different experiences from the discipline that comes with football in itself, the people you are around who are teaching you not only about Xs and Os but about life. That's the type of stuff you have to look into, so it helps you get to the next level. I had to take all of that into account.

"I don't think everyone at Alabama knew. I think the only people who knew were Coach Saban and maybe Coach Smart. It was a surprise. I think my mom told Coach Saban I was leaning that way, but it wasn't a final decision. I was swaying toward Alabama in those final days, but Auburn was still in the back of my mind. It got really bad on Signing Day. I was second-guessing everything. The whole announcement on ESPN was crazy. When I said I was going to Alabama, you really heard all the air just leave the room. People were like, 'Oh shit, that's the place we definitely didn't expect.' From that point it was the birth of the craziness from our end between Alabama and Auburn."

Even Alabama's recruiting coordinator at the time didn't expect Evans to announce for the University of Alabama. "Nobody in the building to my knowledge thought we were getting him," Siskey said. "We had a staff meeting the morning of Signing Day. Everyone was just saying they hadn't heard anything. Then Rashaan picks us. I went down to Coach Saban's office because he doesn't watch or pay attention to any of those announcements. I told him, 'Rashaan just picked us.' He said, 'I know. I was told a few days ago and was told not to tell anyone.' I'm not sure if Kirby knew, but he didn't act like he did."

Lashlee, who had spent more than a year recruiting Evans, believed his recruitment was trending in Alabama's favor despite many believing he would stay in his hometown. "I don't think when you are recruiting a player of Rashaan's caliber you can ever feel like things are in the bag," he said. "We worked really hard to recruit Rashaan and his family. The last two or three months of his recruitment, we really didn't think it was trending in our direction. We didn't think we were getting him on Signing Day. In recruiting when you have these announcements with all the hats and if you don't know before he announces, then you are not getting him. That's just the way it works. It might be one out of every 50 kids who surprises you. Credit to Alabama. They did a good job. It really turned out good for him because he is an awesome player and is killing it in the league."

For Auburn fans Evans became the enemy. "Just the fact I chose Alabama was crazy," he said. "Auburn fans all took that kind of hard. I was born and raised in Auburn. I was truly an Auburn fan growing up. People are wondering, *Why would he not go to Auburn?* When you choose Alabama, it throws people off. I was going over to Auburn all the time. I was hanging out and going to every game. The fans were accustomed to seeing me with other players on the team. It wasn't: who's he going to choose? It was: when is he going to sign? Things changed drastically. I was the enemy now and will be treated accordingly. We really didn't know how much things were going to change."

Evans was recruited by Smart, the former Alabama defensive coordinator who left Tuscaloosa after the linebacker's sophomore season to become the head coach at the University of Georgia. Coach Smart was significant in his recruitment, but Evans credits others from Alabama, too. "I feel like Kirby was the guy I had the best relationship with throughout the process," he said. "He knew my parents really well. He understood me. I felt like everything he said to me was genuine. We just really hit it off. The rest is history. I really think Kirby, Reuben, and Coach Saban all really swayed me to Alabama. It wasn't just one of them. It was a collective effort. Reuben wasn't that hard on me. He would just always lead off with talking about what it would be like if we played together. I always felt like that was intriguing. It was an interesting situation. You have the opportunity to play with a guy who has the same mind-set as you do. He is physical and plays hard. You want to play with other good players who want the same things you do."

That decision impacted the Evans family. "We lost a lot of friends in Auburn because of that," Alan said. "It really changed our lives. We were going to games every weekend at Auburn. We would take Rashaan to the games. Everything revolved around Auburn University football games on Saturdays. We haven't been to an Auburn game since Rashaan left. That's just how drastic things changed. We still live in Auburn, but during the season we are in Nashville or on the road to Chicago or New York, wherever the Titans play. We follow pro football now instead of college. I had a lot of friends, who were really part of the big power stroke at Auburn University: Coach Dye, Jay Jacobs. I felt a lot of pressure from the community. They really wanted Rashaan to go to Auburn University. It was the first time in the history of the school that ESPN came to do a live feed of an announcement. It was a big event. They let all the kids out of school to come to the announcement. You had the whole gym packed. All the teachers and the principal were there. You had all the ESPN cameras. There was a lot of pressure. He made the decision. He pulled out the Alabama hat, and his life changed. My life changed. There are major fallouts from it. Things are better now, but friendships were broken the moment the Alabama hat was pulled out. I know Rashaan doesn't regret his decision. He hasn't looked back one time. I think he made the best decision he could have made."

Evans was a two-time national champion at Alabama and selected in the first round of the NFL draft in 2018. He helped lead the Tennessee Titans to the AFC Championship Game in 2019 before losing to the Super Bowl champion Kansas City Chiefs. As the Titans' starting inside linebacker, he had 111 tackles and 11 tackles for loss during the 2019 season. "I can honestly say it was the best decision I could have ever made," Evans said. "It truly set me up to where I am now. It taught me a lot of things. It molded me to having the mind-set and work ethic that I have and continue to have every day. It taught me to be where your feet are. That's Coach Saban talk right there. Be where your feet are. It's a simple teaching. Be in the moment, especially within the game itself. Don't worry about tomorrow or the past, at least set yourself up where your future will thank you for it."

But his college journey wasn't easy. Times were tough for him when he first arrived in Tuscaloosa. There was a rich amount of talent in the defensive room for Alabama. "It was a tough road to hoe," Alan said. "I have to take my hat off to Rashaan. He is tough. He had to bow his neck up when he got to Alabama. He had to wait his turn. It was tough on him. We had to help keep him in the right frame of mind. I have never seen so much talent on one team as I did when Rashaan first got to Alabama. I've never seen a team so deep on defense. Just about everyone in Rashaan's linebacker room went to the NFL. It was a tremendous amount of talent. They were six, seven deep at every position—not just three deep. He waited his turn. I will say we loved every minute of playing for Coach Saban. They treated Rashaan so good. Coach Cochran, Coach Saban, and Coach Smart did everything they could to make Rashaan the player he is today."

The defensive side of the ball at the time included: Jonathan Allen, Landon Collins, Eddie Jackson, Da'Shawn Hand, Jarran Reed, Ryan Anderson, Reggie Ragland, Reuben Foster, Shaun Dion Hamilton, Tim Williams, and Tony Brown. All are currently in the NFL. "I was never intimidated," Evans said "I always played with older guys growing up. I was already accustomed to playing against that type of competition. I loved competing. Let the best man win. I thrived in that. Alabama was the best place for me because I was able to go up against those type of players every day in practice. Coach Saban is going to get everything out of you: mental, physical, character. He is going to get everything out of you to see if you really want to play football, and if you do really want to play football, how good do you really want to be at it. At Bama you can be a really good football player and develop into an even better man. That's what makes Alabama so special.

"The people at Alabama always showed so much love to Bama players in general. Just having that crimson jersey on, you felt like you were one of the top players in the nation. Alabama had guys like Derrick Henry, Amari Cooper, Mark Ingram, who were all at a rock star status. There was never any drop-off. You go to other schools, and they have players who were good who are enshrined at those programs forever. You come to Alabama and you are part of a huge collection of just really stupid-good players. I loved being a part of that."

Rashaan's younger siblings, Alex and Alexis, attended the University of Alabama, too. He also expects his youngest sister,

Ashley, to attend Alabama. "It's a beautiful thing," Evans said. "You go to a place like Alabama, and it sets you up for things like that to happen. You go to Alabama, you serve your time, you do your job, and you stay out of trouble. When you leave you have the opportunity to help the people, who come behind you, which is your family. That's the great thing about Alabama is they are there for you—not only when you are there but even after. They have a good plan for you for something to be involved in after college. Some guys don't make it to the NFL. Alabama has a Plan B for them. I think Alabama does a great job of helping players find a Plan B. I am happy I was able to provide my family with the opportunity to go to Alabama after I graduated."

CHAPTER 18

Tua Tagovailoa

Tua Tagovailoa is one of the most revered figures in the incredibly rich history of the University of Alabama. His 41-yard touchdown pass to wide receiver DeVonta Smith on second and 26 in overtime in the 2018 College Football Playoff National Championship is forever etched in football history. The play helped capture Nick Saban's fifth national championship with Alabama. It was quite a distinction for a player who came to Alabama from across the map. "Being the first player from Hawaii to commit to Alabama in the past decade is an awesome opportunity for me," Tagovailoa said in May of 2016 from Hawaii. "There are not many kids who get the opportunity to say they are committing to Alabama, the defending national champions. There are a lot of kids in Alabama who don't even get that opportunity. I really just want to extend my gratitude to Coach Saban and Coach Kiffin for the opportunity to commit to Alabama. I told them about a week ago how I felt about the recruiting process. Coach Saban asked how I wanted to do it. We told him we would like to announce it here. He was fine with everything. He wanted us to make it special for the people in Hawaii who have shown so much support and for my family."

Alabama had a tremendous run during the 2015 season after its early loss to Ole Miss, and it ended with Saban's fourth national championship in Tuscaloosa after a 45–40 win against Clemson in Glendale, Arizona. The Tide added a big commitment during the season from Jake Fromm. One of the top junior quarterbacks in the country, he hailed from Houston County High School in Warner Robins, Georgia. Fromm had taken several visits to Alabama and had built a relationship with offensive coordinator Lane Kiffin and area recruiter/defensive coordinator Kirby Smart. But then Smart accepted the head coaching position at the University of Georgia at the conclusion of the season. Smith had committed to the Bulldogs the previous August. "We went up to camp at Georgia for Dawg Night heading into his junior year," Smith's longtime mentor, Vincent Sanders told BamaInsider.com. "It was back when Pruitt and Sam Petitto were up there. I was trying to get him reps with the top group of receivers."

The coaches wouldn't let that happen, but Sanders kept pressing, and finally they relented. "I said, 'Tay, I'm going to be in the back of the end zone. You run, and when you kill them, you bring it all the way to me,'" Sanders said. "He did just that. When he got in the rotation, first play...*boom*. He killed him and brought the ball all the way to me."

Petitto, who served as Georgia's director of player personnel, was a Louisiana native and from the same hometown, Amite City, as Smith. Petitto was hired by Alabama shortly after Coach Smart became the head coach in Athens. Smith re-opened his recruitment in January of 2016. There were other factors involved such as Jeremy Pruitt becoming the defensive coordinator at Alabama. He was the lead recruiter for Smith while in Athens. Georgia also lost its wide receivers coach, Bryan McClendon, to South Carolina. Alabama was considered the frontrunner for Smith after his decommitment from Georgia.

Fromm decided to flip his commitment from Alabama to Georgia on March 3, 2016. Most expected Fromm to flip because of his relationship with Coach Smart. It was not that big of a deal for Kiffin, the offensive coordinator at Alabama back then who is now the head coach at Ole Miss. "We felt pretty good about it," Kiffin said of the quarterback situation. "We really liked Jake. It was a mixed room. I'm not going to say who was on what side. Just like a draft room, it was a mixed room. Kirby was there at the time, and it was Kirby's area. So when Kirby was at Alabama as a position coach, he had Jake's area in Georgia. He had a really good relationship with Jake, and they sent me to go out and watch him practice. Kirby got the job [at Georgia] and started recruiting him, had a good relationship with his family. We were still recruiting him. It was one of those things where we weren't excited about losing him, but we had a good feeling we were getting Tua, so it made it a lot easier. That's why when everyone kept saying when he decommitted it was this big deal, no it wasn't because we basically knew Tua was coming."

Tagovailoa was born March 2, 1998, in Ewa Beach, Hawaii, on the island of Oahu. His parents, Galu and Diane, are originally from American Samoa and raised their family on the Samoan culture more than 4,000 miles away from Tuscaloosa. He is the oldest of four children. Tua was an Oregon fan in his youth because of the fast-paced offense led by former head coaches Chip Kelly and Mark Helfrich, along with Heisman Trophy quarterback Marcus Mariota who had attended the same high school. However, during high school Tua became a big USC fan. He loved watching the quarterbacks, who led the powerhouse offenses, especially Matt Leinart. Tua was a very good high school football player in Hawaii, but how was he going to receive the exposure he needed to become one of the top passers in the country?

Tagovailoa had a strong coming-out party during his sophomore season at St. Louis High School in Honolulu when he completed more than 68 percent of his passes for 2,583 yards with 33 touchdowns and only three interceptions. He also had 576 yards on the ground. Led by then-head coach Steve Sarkisian, USC became the first school to extend an offer after his sophomore season.

Showcase camps and 7-on-7 events have been beneficial to prospects from all across the country to help gain exposure—whether it is someone hoping to garner their first scholarship offer or someone hoping to jump from a three-star to a five-star prospect. Players in Hawaii typically must travel to the mainland to garner attention. George Malauulu is a former quarterback at the University of Arizona and the president of the faith-based AIGA Foundation, which has helped Polynesian players, including Mariota and Pittsburgh Steelers wide receiver JuJu Smith-Schuster, land scholarships since 1997.

Malauulu led a 7-on-7 team at the Las Vegas Pylon 7-on-7 Tournament with two quarterbacks on the roster: Tagovailoa and eighth grade phenom, JT Daniels. Many knew about Daniels, even though he was in eighth grade. He was attending camps in California at a very young age before eventually signing with USC in 2018. (Daniels transferred to Georgia in the spring of 2020.) He also attended Mater Dei High School in Santa Ana, California, the same high school as 2020 Alabama quarterback signee Bryce Young. "Sure enough, people kept looking at our games and were like, 'Who the heck is that?'" Malauulu said. "Everybody knew about JT because JT was the eighth grade phenom. Tua comes out there and he was just lighting up the board. After that event people were talking about Tua. He was able to get some exposure that was well-needed going into his junior year. After that 7-on-7 at Pylon, he had his stamp in the books.

"That throw that you saw that went for the touchdown to win the [title] game, I saw that as a 10ᵗʰ grader. He was 40 yards out. I'm in the back of the end zone with his dad, and all of a sudden, that ball comes, and it's whistling. I was like, *You have to be kidding me.* We're sitting there, getting ready for our next game. As we're getting ready, I tell them you know how we start and how we finish: we start with a prayer and end with a prayer. I asked Tua, 'Tua say the prayer.' This guy, when everybody's eyes are closed, has such a gift on words and showing his passion for his Lord and Savior, Jesus Christ. You would have thought it was an older man talking. He's a once-in-a-lifetime kind of kid."

Recruiting can become so intertwined, and certain situations can alter the course of college football history. Sarkisian (currently the Alabama offensive coordinator) was the head coach at USC from 2014 to 2015. The Trojans were considered the early favorite for Tagovailoa before Coach Sark was fired midseason in 2015. Tagovailoa put forth another outstanding season during his junior year in 2015 with more than 2,900 yards passing and 24 touchdowns. He also had 481 yards rushing and 11 touchdowns. Sarkisian was out as USC's head coach, and lead recruiter, Marques Tuiasosopo, left to become the UCLA passing game coordinator (and is now the tight ends coach at Cal). The door was open for other schools to potentially land Tagovailoa.

It was the spring of Tagovailoa's junior year in high school, and Alabama was coming off a national championship. Fromm flipped to Georgia, and Alabama's quarterback situation had not been determined for the following season as it had four players—Cooper

Bateman, David Cornwell, Blake Barnett, and true freshman Jalen Hurts—competing for the starting role after the departure of Jake Coker. By the time Tagovailoa arrived in Tuscaloosa, it was down to Hurts and freshman Mac Jones. "We kept recruiting him, and he came to us," Kiffin said. "People give me the credit, but Tosh Lupoi had a lot to do with it because we both shared the West Coast, and he did a really good job with the family. We were recruiting him the whole time because you don't know what's going to happen with the kids. We were projecting our numbers to be pretty low that we would potentially take Tua [along with Fromm] in the class. We eventually took two with Tua and Mac Jones."

Tua's father did not believe it at first when Kiffin extended an offer to his son. Once he understood the interest was real, the family made plans as quickly as possible to visit Alabama. The Tagovailoas also took a trip to Auburn during their excursion. "It was great to see all the people and see how big all these campuses are," his father said after the first visit to Alabama. "Just being over at schools like Alabama and Auburn, it was an awesome experience. You can see a big difference in the schools in the South. You can see why things are the way they are at Alabama. I spoke to Lane Kiffin when he offered. We first took it in a way that was not kind of serious. I found it hard to believe they would bypass the whole West Coast and come to the Pacific to look at Tua. I would call and keep making sure he was the guy they wanted. I always want the coaches to see Tua's film. I want them to see the film and know that is who they want. I don't want to put any pressure on coaches. I like to ask them and get their feedback. With Alabama they told me they didn't need to see him in person. His film was good enough. I still wanted them to see him throw before they took his commitment. My wife and I really wanted to visit Alabama and see if it was the place for him. When we got there, it was just like it was back at home. It was like being in Hawaii."

Tua fell in love with Alabama during the first visit in the spring after his junior season. He grew up honoring his parents and following the path they laid out before him. He did not necessarily choose Alabama on his own. He enjoyed the pursuit by the Crimson Tide and the trip to Tuscaloosa, but it was a family decision that led to his commitment to Alabama. His parents decided Alabama was the best choice, even though they knew it would mean leaving behind the life they knew and saying good-bye to friends and family while moving across the country to remain close to Tua during his college career. "First and foremost, the opportunity is small for kids in my position," Tua said when he committed. "They came all the way across the mainland. Not many kids get the opportunity to travel that far to an SEC school like Alabama. If I want to play in the NFL, why not start at a place that runs an NFL type of offense? Why not build your skills up as an NFL talent and prepare yourself at a school that does that for you? If I am blessed to make my dream come true, Alabama is the place that can do that for me."

These were things his father understood regarding the resources, which were available and provided to him at the University of Alabama. The program not only competes for championships on a yearly basis, but it also has state-of-the-art facilities, world-class coaches and training staff, an incredible medical staff, a yearly exodus of talent to the NFL, and the opportunity to play in the best conference in the country. All of those things are available and well-established.

Alabama also brought something more to the Tagovailoas. It brought a great education along with Christian values. He even spent time with former Alabama punter JK Scott (now with the Green Bay Packers) who led a bible study during Tagovailoa's first visit in Tuscaloosa. "I really didn't think I would be committing to Alabama," Tagovailoa said. "I thought it was going to be USC. The environment and the people were so amazing in the South. I have never seen anything like it. They always tell you to go where you feel at home. Alabama felt like home.

"I was there for a week. It was amazing. I got to take a hold and really grasp what the community does on Sundays and on weekdays. I got to see a lot of the football players and coaches go to church. I felt the southern hospitality. They are such grateful and respectful people. It was the biggest thing for me. I wanted to surround myself with people, who are genuine and nice. That's how I was brought up in my community. You really don't want anything more than that."

After committing to Alabama, Tagovailoa became a vocal leader in the Tide's recruiting class. He also remained true to his word and did not take any additional recruiting visits. He was invited to the Elite 11 quarterback camp and walked away as the overall MVP. Sione Ta'ufo'ou is a quarterback mentor and coach on the West Coast. He trained with Tagovailoa a handful of times in Hawaii and California prior to the Elite 11 finals. He also coached there, including guiding Tagovailoa's 7-on-7 team during the Elite 11 finals. "He knows who he is," Coach Ta'ufo'ou said of Tagovailoa. "He's very grounded. He has a great feeling of why he's where he is, and that's his faith. But, two, his ability to manipulate the ball to make all the throws, his timing, and his arm strength—if you combine the person he's become through his parents, the football skillset, his faith in God, his leadership abilities, that's the it factor. That's what makes him special. It's not just that he can throw a football, it's not just that he can make different throws, and he's clutch in different situations, but those guys probably all know that he has their backs. He believes in his faith, and his faith guides him. I remember his transformation from Elite 11 tryouts to Elite 11 finals. He went home and worked on everything, but he came out and did it, and it was flawless. Everything he did at The Opening camp that he struggled with was more like he hadn't been taught how to do it. Then once he was taught how to do it, he went out and did it. That shows you his ability to learn, his ability to transfer information, the discipline to do the lonely work. He knew what was expected and he got it done."

Coach Kiffin knows how important it was for Alabama to land Tagovailoa's signature because it also helped in recruiting other star players in the Tide's No. 1 class in 2017. That class featured offensive stars such as Tagovailoa, Najee Harris, Jerry Jeudy, Henry Ruggs III, Smith, Jedrick Wills, and Alex Leatherwood. All except Wills played a significant amount in Alabama's 26–23 come-from-behind win against Georgia in the national championship as true freshmen. "He helped build that class," Kiffin said. "That opens up nationally recruiting kids to come, so that you can go to Hawaii and get the top quarterback to come to Tuscaloosa. Najee, the running back, sitting out in California. Once you start that, you can kind of piece that together, and then the quarterback usually leads the class. Tua did a good job recruiting that class. He helped those pieces come together, and the biggest relationship was Najee's relationship, and he helped with that."

Tagovailoa passed for 3,932 yards and 43 touchdowns during his senior season in high school. He helped lead St. Louis to the District I State Championship. He finished his career with 8,158 passing yards to rank as the most in Hawaii high school football history. He had 84 total touchdown passes. He also added 1,727 yards and 27 touchdowns on the ground during his three-year career as a starter. He was ranked No. 53 overall in the Rivals100. He participated in the U.S. Army All-American Bowl in San Antonio.

Tagovailoa challenged the reigning SEC Offensive Player of the Year, Hurts, throughout the spring and summer for the starting position. Hurts remained the starter, but Tagovailoa played throughout the year, completing more than 63 percent of his passes for 636 yards, 11 touchdowns, and two interceptions. He was first overall in the SEC in passing efficiency (204.0).

Hurts struggled in the national championship game against the Bulldogs. Alabama was down 13–0 at halftime. Saban made the move to insert Tagovailoa into the game at the start of the third quarter. He engineered an epic comeback with 166 yards passing and three touchdowns, including the walk-off strike to Smith just like Smith had hauled in at Georgia's football camp prior to the start of his junior season in high school.

Tagovailoa was runner-up to Oklahoma quarterback Kyler Murray in the Heisman Trophy race during his sophomore season. He was awarded the Maxwell Award and Walter Camp Award as the nation's best player after passing for 3,966 yards (Alabama record for passing yards in a season) with 43 touchdowns (also an Alabama season record) and only six interceptions during the 2018 season. While accounting for 4,156 yards of total offense, he won the SEC Offensive Player of the Year in 2018, was a consensus All-American, *The Sporting News* Player of the Year, and the Orange Bowl Offensive MVP during a 45–31 win against Oklahoma.

The next year Tagovailoa passed for 2,840 yards with 33 touch-downs and only three interceptions before suffering a season-ending injury in the 10th game of the season against Mississippi State. A week after suffering a 46–41 loss to LSU, the eventual national champion, Tagovailoa was tackled behind the line of scrimmage, causing his hip to dislocate and fracturing the posterior wall. He also suffered a broken nose and concussion.

Alabama fans will remember the great things Tagovailoa did for the University of Alabama. He is remembered for his faith in Jesus Christ and his love for his family, teammates, and coaches. No one will forget the final play of the 2018 national championship against Georgia or when he was carted off the field in his final game with the Crimson Tide. He declared early for the NFL draft after his junior season and was selected fifth overall by the Miami Dolphins.

The Tagovailoas took a leap of faith in leaving Hawaii for a brighter future in college football. Tua's younger brother, Taulia, spent two seasons at Thompson High School in Alabaster, Alabama, before signing with Alabama as one of the top quarterbacks in the country. He played sparingly for the Tide in the 2019 season. He was nine-of-12 for 100 yards, one touchdown, and no interceptions. He transferred to Maryland in the spring after Tua was drafted by the Dolphins.

Competition makes players better, and worrying about who is ahead of them or in the same class was never an issue. "We had a great feeling from what [the Tagovailoas] were saying before Jake decommitted," Kiffin said. "You think they were worried about Jake Fromm? They still came after Jalen Hurts was SEC Offensive Player of the Year as a true freshman. Everybody thought Tua would flip at the end somewhere once Jalen started playing like that. The guy's the first freshman Player of the Year since Hershel Walker. You usually don't follow that because you think you'll sit for three years. Tua's mind-set was different. They still came after that."

Acknowledgments

I want to start by thanking my wife, Audrey, for the unconditional support and love she provides every day. I am beyond lucky to have her in my life. I am also very appreciative of her understanding of the commitment in this profession. Those who work in journalism, especially in the football recruiting industry, don't have the typical 8:00–5:00 job. Some nights we are working until 2:00 AM. Some days she understands why I sleep in. Commitments can happen at any moment. It might be an inconvenience, but we still have to break and/or write the story. Our job isn't a nonstop grind each day, but we are always on-call regardless of the day or time. My wife understands it. She doesn't mind the phone resting on the dinner table or having to pause a favorite show for a minute in order for me to speak with a player or coach. I am beyond blessed to have her in my life and love her with all of my heart.

I also want to thank my parents, who have supported and believed in me from Day One. I didn't know where this recruiting journey would take me when I accepted a paid internship when I was a freshman at the University of Alabama in 2003. I thought it was just some extra money to have while I was in college. My parents kept encouraging me. It was my first real job. I always assumed I would go into the family real-estate business after college. I was never pressured to do that. My parents always wanted me to find my own path; maybe it would lead me to the real-estate world. I am a real-estate broker, but it was my decision later in life. I stayed on the path as a recruiting reporter, and it has opened many doors. I'm so appreciative of my parents for all they have done for me.

There are many others who helped me get to the point where I am now. Scott Kennedy, who hired me to work for him at Scout.com in 2003. Kirk McNair, who trusted an 18 year old without much writing experience to write a column for his *Bama Magazine*. I also want to thank *The Tuscaloosa News*/TideSports.com for hiring me when I was only 21 years old. I spent several years writing a column every Tuesday for the newspaper. I also want to give a special thanks to the former head of Rivals.com, Eric Winter. Eric flipped my commitment from Scout.com to Rivals.com in 2012. It was a major moment in my life and rejuvenated my love for the profession. I was at a crossroads in my life—trying to decide if I was going to continue as a recruiting reporter or change my career. Eric made me feel like the No. 1 priority for him in his first year as the head of Rivals.com. I joined the Alabama team site. Some changes were made with the Alabama site a few years down the road, and I had to make a tough decision to either remain with Rivals or *The Tuscaloosa News*/TideSports.com. I remained with Rivals and launched a new Alabama site. I can't thank Kyle Henderson (managing editor of BamaInsider.com) and Gene Williams enough for their effort in keeping me on board. BamaInsider.com is a tremendous website dedicated to covering Alabama athletics. I lead the charge on the football recruiting landscape. I hope you all will consider joining our site and become a part of our online community of Crimson Tide fans!

I, of course, have to give a special shout-out to my best friends. I am not going to name them individually. You all know who you are because you are reading this right now. You all have been there with me through thick and thin. Thank you all for the support you always give me and all the great times we have on a regular basis. Many of you I see each week. Many live out of town, and I wish we could spend more time together, but I am thankful for all of you in my life.

This book could not have been written without all of the former Alabama *greats*, who let me interview them throughout the last year. There are 100-plus Alabama greats, who I wanted to spotlight. The Alabama football tradition and history are unparalleled. I have friends, who played at Alabama, I wish I could have included. I hope to write another book in the future to feature other Alabama greats I had originally contacted, who are not part of this book. I had to trim the list somehow, and it was extremely difficult. Some of these players were childhood heroes of mine. I covered some during their recruitment. Brodie Croyle and I played high school football together. Some were players who I knew about growing up because my parents made sure I knew about how great those guys were during their younger years.

I was blown away to speak on the phone to so many legends in Alabama football history. Some were certainly much harder than others to track down. I had a lot of help from various people— friends, Alabama contacts, and even former players, who helped me at least get a phone number or email address. I can't thank those people enough!

It was one of the greatest honors of my life to interview all of these players as they talked about their life growing up and becoming a football star. I was beyond excited to speak on the phone with several parents, former high school coaches, mentors, and opposing coaches who recruited the players to their school. It meant the world to me to speak on the phone with former Alabama head coach Gene Stallings. I was a month away from turning 8 years old when Alabama won the national championship against Miami on January 1, 1993. It's the time period when you really start to remember everything rather than just bits and pieces. I remember going crazy a month prior during the inaugural SEC Championship Game in Birmingham when Antonio Langham intercepted Shane Matthews. We even had a cat named Langham back then. I can now call Antonio a friend, and he was also a vital piece in helping me get a few guys on board with this book.

I was very fortunate to have Triumph Books contact me to write this book. I've had many people say to me, "You should write a book because of all the years as a recruiting reporter." I imagined I would eventually write a book on the Shula/Saban years. I never imagined I would have the opportunity to interview guys like Lee Roy Jordan, Cornelius Bennett, Johnny Musso, Marty Lyons, David Palmer, John Hannah, Chris Samuels, and DeMeco Ryans about their life and recruiting journey. I was fortunate to know Jay Barker, Langham, Dwight Stephenson, Croyle, and Bobby Humphrey. It was amazing to speak with them about their experience and learn the twists and turns of their recruitment. I covered the recruitments of Tua Tagovailoa, Barrett Jones, Trent Richardson, Rashaan Evans, and T.J. Yeldon. It was awesome to put their story together and showcase how their journey to Tuscaloosa unfolded. I want to thank Tom VanHaaren who wrote, *The Road to Ann Arbor*. He provided guidance and assistance. I am so appreciative of my editor, Jeff Fedotin. I am sure he spent a ton of time editing mistakes throughout each chapter. He was such a great person to work with throughout the process.

I want to thank my wife's entire family. It's a big one! I am so blessed to have you all in my life. I love being an uncle, brother in-law, son-in-law, grandson-in-law to all of you. I hit the jackpot with my in-laws. I also want to thank the Bone and Campbell family for everything they have meant to me throughout my life.

I was born in Tuscaloosa. I lived across the street from Calvary Baptist Church until I was 7 years old. My entire family and I went to school at the University of Alabama. Luckily, my wife and her entire family did as well. I am five years older than she, and we didn't meet until we were both out of college. It didn't stop me from getting her number at Gallettes in 2016 after the Alabama–Mississippi State game. Alabama football has been part of my life since I was born. I cover the best football program in the country. I have attended seven national championship games, of which Alabama won five. I am glad I grew up in a state/cover a team where football is so important. It has given me a career. A career which I truly love and enjoy!

Audrey and I live in Homewood, Alabama. We love hitting the road to Bama on Fridays in the fall with our Cavapoo, Louie, and our diabetic cat, Mac. I am shocked I completed my first book and hope you all enjoy reading about all of these former players as much as I enjoyed writing about them. Roll Tide!

Sources

RollTide.com

Rivals.com

Sports Illustrated

BamaInsider.com

The Tuscaloosa News

DallasCowboys.com

AHSFHS.org

ASHOF.org

ProfootballHOF.com

CBS Sports

Montgomery Advertiser

The Birmingham News

AL.com

The Last Coach

Lee Roy: My Story of Faith, Family, and Football

PalmerWilliamsGroup.org

BaylorSchool.org

NFL.com

Sun-Sentinel

WalterCamp.org
DwightStephenson.org
MartyLyonsFoundation.org
NewYorkJets.com
CFBHall.com
Chicago Tribune
DenverBroncos.com
Redskins.com
BigOak.org
UA.edu